BIODYNAMIC PASTURE MANAGEMENT

BIODYNAMIC PASTURE MANAGEMENT

Balancing Fertility, Life & Energy

Peter Bacchus

ACRES U.S.A.
Austin, Texas

BIODYNAMIC PASTURE MANAGEMENT
© 2013 by Peter Bacchus

All rights reserved. No part of this book may be used or reproduced without written permission except in cases of brief quotations embodied in articles and books.

The information in this book is true and complete to the best of our knowledge. All recommendations are made without guarantee on the part of the author and Acres U.S.A. The author and publisher disclaim any liability in connection with the use or misuse of this information.

Cover photography © Thinkstock
Page 10 photography © Thinkstock

Acres U.S.A.
P.O. Box 301209
Austin, Texas 78703 U.S.A.
512-892-4400 • fax 512-892-4448
info@acresusa.com • *www.acresusa.com*

Manufactured in the United States of America

Peter Bacchus, 1940-
Biodynamic pasture management / Peter Bacchus. Austin, TX, ACRES U.S.A., 2013
xxii, 147 pp., 23 cm.
Includes index
ISBN 978-1-60173-039-8

1. Agriculture — organic   2. Pastures — management   3. Soil fertility.
I. Bacchus, Peter, 1940-   II. Title.

SB318.B33 2013   633.2

I would like to dedicate this book to
my late mother and father, George and Nancy Bacchus,
who facilitated my early learning of biodynamics.
They enthused me to make it a lifetime study.

ACKNOWLEDGEMENTS

I would like to express my gratitude firstly to my parents, George and Nancy Bacchus, for instilling in me knowledge and respect for biodynamic methods. Also to my wife, Gill, but for whom this book would not have been written.

Thank you to Glen Atkinson for many stimulating and expanding discussions on matters pertaining to biodynamics; to Ray, Jenny and Grant Ridings and Yvonne and James Killalea, the farmers who put my management suggestions into practice and provided me with photos. Also to Janet Perrett who gave me helpful feedback on how my suggestions worked in practice, and to Steve and Jenny Erickson for sharing ideas and biodynamic preparation making. Thank you to Mike Chapman for allowing me to demonstrate the effects of biodynamic preparations on his farm.

Thank you to Anne Van Nest and Fred Walters at Acres U.S.A. for putting this book together; they have been a pleasure to work with.

Contents

INTRODUCTION
xi

1. THE MARKET HAS SPOKEN
1

2. DOES THE FOOD YOU PRODUCE
CONTRIBUTE TO HEALTH?
5

3. ORGANIC SOIL FERTILITY, SOIL BIOLOGY
& WHOLE FARM MANAGEMENT
13

4. SOIL MINERAL BALANCE
23

5. NITROGEN AND OXYGEN IN PLANT GROWTH
& OVERCOMING LEACHING PROBLEMS
39

6. BIODYNAMIC SYSTEMS FOR NEW WORLD FARMERS
47

7. CALCIUM , SILICA & BD PREP 500 AND 501
57

8. BIODYNAMICS & BUILDING ORGANS
69

9. BIODYNAMIC COMPOST PREPARATIONS: COMPOST, WORM FARMS & BARREL MANURE
77

10. WEED MANAGEMENT & PLANT PEPPERING
93

11. USING BIODYNAMICS TO MANAGE PESTS & DISEASE, ANIMAL PEPPERING
103

12. ANIMAL HEALTH MANAGEMENT
113

13. DAIRY FARM EFFLUENT MANAGEMENT
123

14. IT IS BEING DONE
Successful Biological & Biodynamic Growing with High Yields and Profit
129

15. HOW BIODYNAMICS & MINERAL BALANCING COULD TRANSFORM FARMING AND THE FOOD SUPPLY IN THE FUTURE
135

RESOURCES
138

INDEX
143

Introduction

At an early age my parents instilled in me the understanding that peoples' health related closely to the health of the soil and the environment in which their food was grown. I grew up with this concept. My parents were both strongly convinced that biodynamic farming produced healthier food, although I didn't take any interest in biodynamics until I was about 22 years old.

My mother's aunt and uncle, Rachel and Bernard Crompton Smith, traveled from New Zealand to Europe in 1927 to learn about Rudolf Steiner's teachings. They brought back to New Zealand the first initiatives of biodynamics and Waldorf education. The biodynamic orchard they developed in Havelock North on the North Island's Hawke's Bay region has long since been replaced by houses, but the oak tree they grew to provide bark for one of the biodynamic preparations still stands.

My father always wanted to be a farmer but his father compelled him to take an engineering degree at university. He finally broke loose and travelled to Germany in 1933 to study biodynamics. He was taught by Max Karl Schwarz who ran a school near Bremerhaven. Then he was apprenticed to farmer Ernst Stegemann who was a prime mover in persuading Rudolf Steiner to give the "Agriculture Course" which provided the basis for biodynamics.

I was born in the United Kingdom where my parents went to advise on biodynamic principles and techniques. We returned to New Zealand after the second World War when I was six years old. I grew up on my parent's dairy farm in Wharepoa near Paeroa, just southeast of Auckland, New Zealand.

The link between the soil and human health was brought home to me by an early experience. When I was in my early thirties, I became very thin and withdrawn, could not stand the light, needed reading glasses, and almost had a nervous breakdown. I intuitively realized that these were symptoms of a lack of phosphorus. My father and I had applied plenty of the biodynamic preparation (BD) 500 over many years on the dairy farm that I took over from him. This preparation stimulates soil microbial life, which is able to absorb then release phosphorus, making it available for plant growth. Phosphorus tends to be in short supply in New Zealand soils, and after a number of years the supply in the soil had run out. That was before the days when farms regularly had soil tests done and before organic soil amendments such as rock phosphate were available. My mother, as farm owner, would not allow superphosphate on the farm. The other thing that would have helped to reduce this phosphorus imbalance was the biodynamic preparation 501, but in those days we were nervous about using it because if it was applied at the wrong time it could result in depressed pasture growth.

The author feeding willow twigs to weaner calves.

Since that time I have come to realize the importance of having all the minerals needed for plant growth properly balanced in the soil. I have studied mineral balancing as introduced in the United States by Dr. William A. Albrecht and subsequently taught by Arden Andersen, Phil Wheeler and others as basis for the biological farming method. Many farmers in the United States, Australia and New Zealand have adopted this farming method that builds healthy soil with flourishing soil organisms, producing healthy plants and nutrient-dense food.

Balancing minerals in the soil is also important for the health of animals grazing on the pastures and people living on the homegrown vegetables, meat and milk that are produced by the farm. The farm is a living entity. As the farmer carries the identity of the farm, his health will naturally be influenced by the health of the farm and conversely the farm's health is influenced by the health of the farmer.

There is growing evidence about the links between diet and food nutritional quality and many diseases such as cancer, cardiovascular disease, attention deficit syndrome and even criminal behavior. The progressive deterioration of health over generations that Rudolf Steiner warned about is still not generally recognized. I think we will see a dramatic increase in serious childhood disease as a result of the bad diets of their grandparents. In the United States, Dr. Arden Andersen, reports that many of the children coming to him for treatment of serious health problems such as cancers, food allergies and skin disease can be helped, or even cured, by an improved diet.

There is still a perception among the majority of farmers that organic and biodynamic farming are not profitable options. I challenge anyone with that view to read on and learn about some organic farmers who are already farming very profitably. Farmers can maintain a very comfortable lifestyle using a combination of approaches and techniques developed by organic and biodynamic farmers using modern scientific knowledge about balancing the soil minerals required for optimum biological farming. Besides a comfortable lifestyle, this combination of approaches and techniques can also provide really nutritious food to improve and sustain the health of the people who consume their products.

This book aims to give practical guidance and useful tips to those who have stewardship over the land — those who believe that they belong to the land as much as the land belongs to them, people who nurture the soil, plants and animals as well as they nurture themselves.

I
The Market Has Spoken

In the late 1980s I was living in Hawkes Bay, New Zealand, and at the time was very much concerned that the overseas market for New Zealand apples would not continue to accept food products grown using large quantities of horticultural sprays which were being used to "protect" the products from harm. Sensing a global shift was happening, I felt I had to change my growing system in order to maintain market access.

One of the ways I aimed to assist this "reduced toxic input" change was to develop a commercial supply of compost to sell to apple growers. The compost would improve biological activity in the soil which would help to make the apple trees more resilient to pests and disease. Unfortunately my venture into large-scale compost production, one of the first in New Zealand, did not flourish as I ran into various supply difficulties. Even today, now that there is more large-scale compost being made in the country, I still do not see much good compost being used, and in my mind, bad compost can be worse than no compost at all.

Well, fifteen years after my prediction, the market had spoken and by 2006 many of the Hawkes Bay apple trees had been pulled out, in spite of grower investment in new varieties. The few apple growers who had converted to an organic system, though, still had highly profitable operations. For example, Te Koha Orchard near Havelock North produces high-quality, Demeter-certified, biodynamic apples for export and local markets. In Europe and the United States the growing demand for high-quality food has led to an increasing number of farmers growing for local markets such as for farmers' markets and community-supported agriculture (CSA).

The corn-fed beef grown in feedlots has come under increasing criticism — it is quite a different product from pasture-fed beef. Pioneers like Joel Salatin have shown that integrated, more natural systems, as demonstrated on Polyface Farm in Virginia, are viable.

Most domestic cattle, where European civilization has spread, have taken European plants and animals with them. For these plants and cattle to do well and produce high-quality food, soils often need to be adapted to resemble the high-calcium, high-humus soils, and above ground environments found across much of Europe. There all our domestic grazing animals naturally grazed and browsed on mixed shrubby grasslands, where they found food, shelter and medicine. Wherever you go in the world farmers need to adapt the environment, soil and plant species to the needs of the animals being raised.

Many wine growers in New Zealand and Europe are finding that biodynamic practices are helping them to produce top-quality wine. James and Annie Millton near Gisborne, New Zealand have used biodynamic methods to enhance the flavors and emphasize the "terroir" that makes their wines distinctive.

Some organic livestock farmers have found customers in New Zealand cities who are happy to pay higher prices for their products, such as lamb sausages from Marama Organic Farm and yogurt from Clearwater's Organic Dairy. The biodynamic pork produced by the Loch Arthur Community in Camphill, Scotland is highly regarded by customers.

There has been a lot of research comparing organic and biodynamic systems with soluble fertilizer farming. Overall the results have not been very conclusive. This is because there are so many variables and the way a farmer adapts the system to suit his particular farm circumstances is more important than following any particular recipe. Any comparisons are dependent on what is measured. Many people and most animals have no trouble telling the difference. The science will no doubt catch up in due course. The farmers and growers I know (and mentioned above) have found that biodynamic methods have assisted them to produce food that their customers acclaim as high quality.

These people are getting on with caring for their land and putting biodynamics into practice. I feel that it is important to get going with it and get it done rather than to wait for research to prove conclusively it is the right path to take.

Demand for high-quality food has increased as people realize the connection between the food they eat and their health. Our preferences for food is set early in life and is one of the great responsibilities of parenting. It has been more and more frequently observed that what we eat before and during our childbearing years affects not only our health, but that of our children, grandchildren and great-grandchildren. Such far reaching effects were shown in the cat experiments done by Francis M. Pottenger, M.D. in the 1940s. Over 10 years, Pottenger used 900 cats to determine what effects processed foods have on the body and whether there was a degenerative disease trait passed along from generation to generation.

We now know that eating high-quality food not only reduces incidence of conditions such as cancer and heart disease, but also improves immune systems, male sperm counts, and our behavior and thinking.

In Europe, consumers want not only good quality but also to know where their food comes from. They want assurance that their food has been produced with minimal damage to the environment, wild plants and animals. Farmers' markets where local producers sell their own high-quality produce have become widespread in this region. Germany has a long tradition of *reformhauser*, health food stores where the best food can be bought. Farmers' markets are also becoming popular in many other parts of the world as consumers seek locally grown food.

A problem in New Zealand and many other countries is that many people still want to buy cheap food. This reduces a farmers' incentive to produce high-quality products for the local market and consumers get what they pay for — lower quality food. Luckily, there is a growing number of people who see the value of healthy food and will pay for this quality.

Successful biological and organic growers have found that if they look after their soil and produce in a sustainable way they don't have the high costs incurred by growers using a lot of chemicals. Most organic dairy farmers have reduced their animal health veterinary bills considerably because their cows are now healthier. It also costs no more to ship high-quality products than it does to transport second-rate products, and the value is higher.

If farmers had to pay for the environmental damage they cause, for example, the damage from escaping nitrates and phosphorus into streams, rivers and coastal waters, good organic farmers would be very well rewarded indeed, or perhaps chemical farmers would soon be out of business. We currently pay for cheap food with extra taxes and reduced fish stock in polluted streams, rivers and coastal waters — many of which have become unusable for recreation.

2

Does the Food You Produce Contribute to Health?

Consider the following questions about your livestock …

How healthy are your animals?
Do their coats shine and their eyes sparkle?
How often do your animals get sick?
Do you have to feed a lot of mineral supplements and medicines to keep your livestock healthy? Why is this when some farmers hardly ever see their veterinarians, their vet bills are low, and their animals are thriving.

How about yourself?
Do you wake up in the morning feeling that you can move mountains or do you drag yourself out of bed, dreading the coming day with so many things to do?

Scientists are finding more and more connections between nutrition and health. They are also finding connections between the content and quality of the diet with behavior and psychological problems. The evidence shows that you can improve your health through what you eat. This also applies to your animals — you can improve your livestock health through good nutrition.

I will always remember the tale about the very poor woman in a village near Bremerhaven, Germany, who was observed buying fruit and vegetables for her family from the most expensive, high-quality stall in the market. When asked how she could afford to buy this expensive food she said, "This food is more economical than cheap food. I can feed my family with less of it because it is more satisfying, and as it keeps them healthy I don't have doctors' fees."

Have you thought lately about your goals for your farm? Obviously you need to make a profit as you are operating a business, but do you also have an easy system that enables you to have a good quality of life as well as operate a business? Look around — is your staff happy, challenged, and staying with you for long periods?

Many people suffer digestive problems and some are diagnosed with "leaky gut syndrome." With this disease, nutrients from the food that we eat have not been properly digested and are leaked out of the gut into the body where they can do damage. Many modern farms have "leaky" systems too where some of the nutrients volatize into the air or leach out of the soil, pollute the groundwater, and deprive plants of the nutrients they need. To produce food that does not lead to problems such as inflammation and leaky gut syndrome we need farms that are not leaky and retain all the right nutrients to produce good food.

Farming in a sustainable way is less stressful than intensive chem-

One of the true goals of building healthy soil is to raise healthy cattle.

ical farming — you have time to enjoy it. And this is important for producing high-quality food. In talking to a dairy farmer friend about this, he said he has little work to do these days except milking his cows. His father had the foresight to plant plenty of trees on the property which provide a nice shady, sheltered environment. My dairy farmer friend amended his soil to balance the soil minerals and encourage soil organisms to thrive many years ago. He also established medicinal herbs so that his cows could self-medicate themselves when necessary. So now the farm looks after itself, growing excellent pasture that feeds healthy cows.

Keep smiling (like a banana the right way up); this will affect the plants and animals around you. Masaru Emoto, the Japanese author and entrepreneur, has demonstrated the effect of one's mood and thoughts on water around you. His studies show that happy loving thoughts result in water that freezes into beautiful crystals, whereas unhappy, and or hateful thoughts produce deformed patterns.[1] Since we humans and the plant and animal life around us are largely made up of water, consider how your thoughts can have a big effect. Our thoughts are part of the quality process. Loving your soil, plants and animals and realizing that what you are doing is all an important part of making food that is fit to eat.

Repeated observations in North America and Europe have found that children at schools where most of them have a good organic diet are healthier, more amenable to teacher instruction, enjoy learning, and learn more than children in schools who do not generally have such a healthy diet.

To improve livestock health involves improving the quantity and quality of protein and essential oils in the pasture and forage they eat. Many of the recommendations I make to farmers are aimed at this goal. Improving essential oil content not only improves livestock health, but also raises the beneficial omega-3 fatty acid content of milk and meat products.

---

1 Emoto, Masaru , *The Hidden Messages in Water*, (2004), Beyond Words Publishing Inc., Oregon.

FOOD NEEDS TO CONTAIN:

All the necessary minerals in the right proportion.

Research has shown that there has been a decline in levels of minerals in our fruit and vegetables over the last 60 years.[2]

The use of NPK fertilizers results in unbalanced mineral uptake, and lower uptake of trace elements by crop plants and pasture, so some trace elements are often deficient.

Plenty of vitamins and antioxidant activity.

Our food needs to be fresh and ripened and cooked carefully to retain its vitamins. Some cooking techniques can preserve or reduce the loss of vitamins and antioxidants. Also organic products have been found to contain more antioxidants than those grown with soluble fertilizers.[3]

Complex sugars.

Complex sugars are formed when the plant is able to use the sunlight in the right balance and intensity. When a plant is forced to take up a lot of soluble nitrogen quickly or when there is inadequate sunlight, the plant is unable to convert much of the simple sugars into complex sugars. Fruit that is left to ripen on the tree contains a lot of complex sugars.

Protein containing essential amino acids in the right balance.

Good protein is formed when there is plenty of light activity, when the plant contains sufficient magnesium, silica and phosphorus and when calcium, potassium and nitrate are in the right balance.

When there is plenty of biological activity around plant roots, they

---

[2] Mayer, Anne-Marie, "Historical changes in the mineral content of fruits and vegetables: a cause for concern?" Agricultural Production and Nutrition Conference, (1997), Boston, Massachusetts.

[3] Ren, Huifeng, Hideaki Endo, Tetsuhito Hayashi, "Antioxidative and antimutagenic activities and polyphenol content of pesticide-free and organically cultivated green vegetables using water-soluble chitosan as a soil modifier and leaf surface spray." Journal of the Science of Food and Agriculture, (December, 2001), Vol. 81, Issue 15, 1426-1432.

can take up amino acids made by microorganisms instead of just taking up soluble nitrates. It is important to regulate the quantity of nitrates taken in by plants and to make sure plants are sufficiently activated by sunlight to convert nitrates to protein. Cattle can die from nitrate poisoning when nitrites (converted by the digestion process from nitrates in forage) are formed that block the transport of oxygen in the blood, causing asphyxiation of the muscles — including the heart muscle.

Unsaturated essential oils with the right ratio of omega-3 to omega-6 fatty acids.
Animals fed high-quality pasture produce milk and meat high in omega-3 fatty acids and those animals are healthier than animals fed pasture or grain with a high nitrate content.

It is important to consider the life and integrity of the whole food. It should taste, smell, feel and look right with good ranges of colors and subtle flavors. Good-quality food with a high protein content should leave you feeling happy and satisfied. If you are feeling after a meal, "Well, that was good but now where's the real food?" then clearly the food in your meal was not good enough. Animals can tell the difference — in a good-quality paddock they eat more and trample less. A farmer friend I know uses a "drive-by test" to assess his pasture quality. A few hours after he puts his cows in a paddock, he drives by to see them grazing. If they ignore him the pasture must be satisfactory, but if they bellow and run after him, he knows they are looking for some better grass.

In these days when products are minutely analyzed it is important to remember that the whole determines the parts. There are various tests for food quality that look at the integrity of the whole product, such as delayed luminescence, infrared, chromatography, or rapid crystallization. But the best scientists in my mind have four legs and a fur coat — if you give animals a choice they will select the best-quality food available. They have extremely sensitive noses and palates.

In the preface written by Ehrenfried Pfeiffer to the 1974 edition of Rudolf Steiner's *Agriculture Course,* Pfeiffer relates how he asked Steiner why the people to whom Steiner was giving a lot of spiritual

A cow's nose is very sensitive. The best scientist in the world has four legs and a furcoat.

guidance to in turn showed so little spiritual progress. Steiner replied that it was a problem of nutrition. "Nutrition as it is today does not supply the strength necessary for manifesting the spirit in physical life. A bridge can no longer be built from thinking to will and action. Good nutrition is vital in the enabling of sound thinking and the connection of thought and deeds. Food plants no longer contain the forces people need for this." Amazingly, Steiner said this around 1924, decades before the introduction of fast food and the intensification of agriculture that we have today.[4]

My observation is that when we have the whole organism of our farm or garden balanced in every respect, plants are much better able to find the nutrition they need. Many farmers have noticed that the behavior of their animals changes according to the quality of their nutrition. I have heard a farmer comment that a neighbor's herd was

---

4 Steiner, Rudolf, *Agriculture*, (1974), Biodynamic Agricultural Association, London, United Kingdom.

screaming with stomach ache while his next door were satisfied and content. Another commented that cows that in the past were in a hurry to move after two days in a paddock, were quite happy with the same amount of fodder after three days. When the energy balance and flow are right, better nutrition is achieved.

3

Organic Soil Fertility, Soil Biology & Whole Farm Management

To grow healthy plants and animals and high-quality food products you need fertile soil. Soil fertility in turn is related to the growth and reproduction of soil organisms and to the plants that grow in the soil. In due process this affects the health, well-being and fertility of the animals and humans who live as a result of the plants that grow in the soil. We often do not recognize that soil fertility depends on the carbon cycle, which starts with photosynthesis in plant leaves and the absorption of light and carbon and other elements from the air into the plant. The carbon taken in from the air by plants and transformed into sugars is the basis of the carbon cycle, which maintains life in the soil by providing food for soil organisms. The elements that come from the air in gaseous form can make up to 80 percent of solid plant tissue. And up to 90 percent of a plant is carbon and oxygen, two elements that are not measured in many plant tests. What is below ground helps make it to happen.

One of the most often overlooked aspects in our farming is soil biology. Soil organisms are the facilitators of mineral activity in the soil. They bring about a natural movement of minerals through incorporating them in their bodies. These organisms secrete digestive enzymes into the soil that enable the organisms to absorb the minerals as food. When the organisms die, the minerals are released in a form that plant roots can easily take up.

The payment these organisms exact for doing this work is a requirement for the right living conditions and some nutrition. And we can help achieve these requirements. The organisms need air and moisture —

but not too wet or too dry. They work best in a particular temperature range and similar to humans, need food to their liking. Not only do they need organic matter, they need a specific range of mineral nutrients. They can't hop in the car or bus and go to the supermarket and pharmacy — they depend on us and our animals to deliver the goods.

The bacteria need sugars that they get from root exudates. Some of the sap that carries the sugars created by photosynthesis down to the roots is exuded into the soil. As sunlight enables the photosynthesis through which sugars are made by plants, the soil organisms are fed indirectly by sunlight. The mineral balance and health of the plant affects the quality of sugars exuded from plant roots. For example, the element magnesium is needed by the plant to assist this photosynthesis process, and other elements, such as boron, assist the plant to move the sugars down to the roots and the soil nutrients up into the plant.

Animals and humans should obtain what they need from plants, and these plants should obtain what they need from the soil, air and light, rather than feeding minerals directly to animals and humans. When we try to take short cuts to speed things up, trouble may lurk and it often ends up being the long way round as well as the wrong way round. In this circle of life there are no free lunches and everything has to work for its living. Human intervention is part of this cycle and to get our "lunch" we need to do our bit with sensitivity and understanding. Our first commandment for farmers, as in medicine, should be, "do no harm."

ENERGY CYCLES & THE SOIL FOOD WEB

Sunshine begins the energy cycle and enables the plant to form sugars, taking carbon and oxygen from the air and hydrogen from the water. Carbon, hydrogen and oxygen are the main constituents of sugar. The plant shares some of the sugars with the roots, mycorrhizal fungi and soil bacteria. Most beneficial soil organisms are aerobic, breathing nitrogen and oxygen from the air that contributes to the protein they build. Soil organisms feed other organisms of different species in a continuous cycle described by Dr. Elaine Ingham in the *Soil Biology*

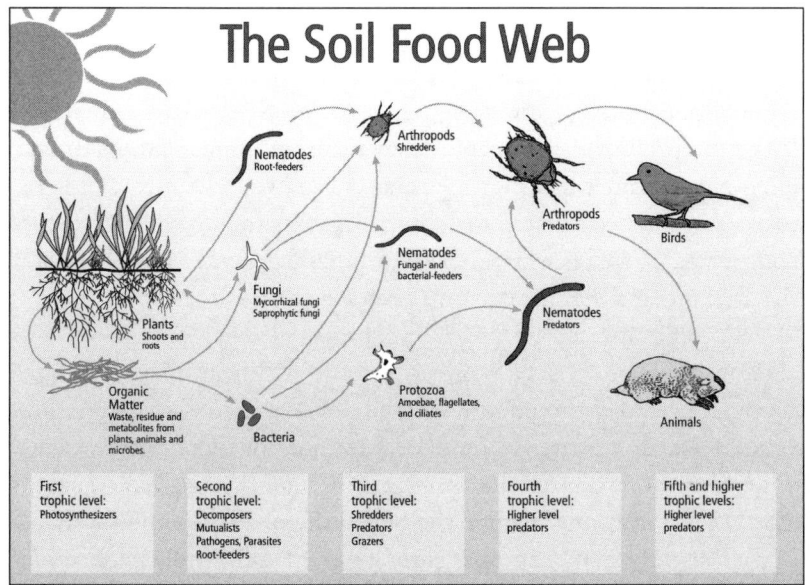

Relationships between soil foodweb, plants, organic matter, and birds and mamals. Image courtesy of USDA Natural Resources Conservation Service.

Primer as the soil food web.[1] Some scientists can spend a lifetime studying one or two species of one soil organism group. Dr. Ingham has identified 25,000 different soil organisms, and when she stopped counting it wasn't that she had run out of organisms, but that she had more important things to do. Soil microbiologists say that only about 2 percent of all the different soil organisms have been identified and given names.

What is surplus to these organisms in the soil is made available to the plants along with other minerals held in the soil. The energy cycle is long and involved, and where every living thing is fed and watered and contributes to the growth of other organisms.

Bacteria that cluster around the roots help protect plants from other organisms that would attack their roots. Bacteria are the beginning of the food chain in the soil. Many of them use the finely ground rocks that contain essential elements as the raw materials of soil life. They also need sufficient organic material to feed on and eventually they are

---

[1] Elaine Ingham, *Soil Biology Primer* (2000), Soil and Water Conservation Society, USDA Natural Resources Conservation Service, p. 5.

eaten by other organisms. Bacteria have the highest protein content of all soil organisms, so when they are eaten by other organisms, such as nematode worms, some nitrogen is given off — as the nematodes don't need it all. This nitrogen is then available for plant roots to take up. When a farmer can manage this process well, the nitrogen is released at a rate that plants can take up, rather than having an excess being available that is wasted and may pollute ground water. The plant can then process the nitrates into proteins.

The protein formed in the plant contains nitrogen and sulfur. This added to the elements, carbon, oxygen and hydrogen make up sugar. Sunlight provides the energy for the development from sugar and nitrate to quality protein. There are a number of sugar forms as well as many forms of protein. In my opinion the more complex the sugars and proteins that are formed, the better the quality of the fodder or food. Plants that contain only simple sugars and nitrates are fodder for plant pests, which are usually simple organisms. Plants need to develop complex sugars and proteins to provide fodder suitable for animals and humans to eat.

However, if the plant takes up too much soluble nitrate at once it cannot turn it all into protein, particularly in dreary weather, and the nitrate in the grass becomes a problem for the animal that eats it. Nitrates can turn into nitrites which inhibit good digestion and the movement of oxygen in animal blood and muscle.

Much of the nitrogen that plant roots take up is in the form of nitrates. Nitrates contain three parts oxygen and one part nitrogen. Nitrates carry oxygen into the plant and this oxygen may be more important than the nitrogen. The pore spaces in soil created by active biology enable the soil to hold more air that can sustain plant growth into cooler, wetter weather periods. Air contains oxygen that is vital to all living things as well as being the most active paramagnetic element on the earth. To get good root growth the soil needs a paramagnetic element. Where there is oxygen, aerobic organisms are encouraged, while the pathogens that are usually anaerobes are greatly diminished. If air and moisture are not in the correct ratios in soil pores there is insufficient oxygen and moisture for the beneficial bacteria and fungi, so the pathogenic organisms tend to develop. Pathogenic organisms

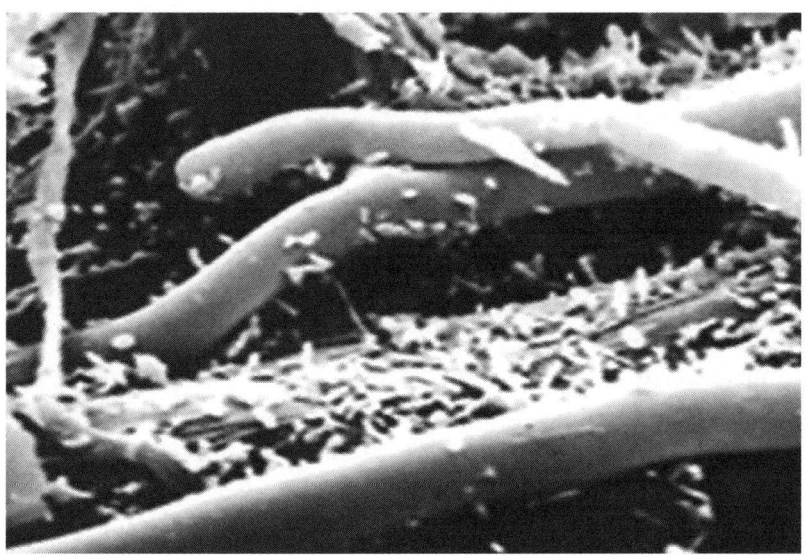
Healthy mycorrhyzal fungi are key to healthy pastures.

can breed many times faster than those we consider to be beneficial to the crops we wish to grow. It is therefore most important that we create the right conditions in the soil to achieve our objectives.

Fungi are another primary organism type in the soil. Some varieties are involved in the breakdown of woody material and dry stalks into soil-releasing nutrients. Another important type is the mycorrhizal fungi which attach themselves to plant roots where they receive sustenance from the plant and in return draw in nutrients from beyond the reach of the plants roots. Mycorrhizal fungi play a key role in collecting up phosphorus and calcium for plant roots. If soil biology is not working properly, these elements remain locked up in the soil. The fungi are able to hold phosphorus and calcium until the plant needs them.

When you think that each of these species has a specific role in nutrient cycling in the soil, it shows how difficult it would be to replace soil biology with soluble fertilizers and get it right. Nature knows best! In our time of climate change and weather extremes, it is very important to have a large diversity of soil biology that can provide flexibility. If you have a range of species, each of which functions at a different temperature or water table level, your pasture can keep growing in a much wider range of weather conditions than pasture that is depending on a few species of biology or on soluble fertilizers.

In order for nutrients to be released by soil organisms at the rate that pasture plants can take them up, it is important to have a well-balanced population of the various types and species of soil organisms. Otherwise you can get a lot of release at the wrong time and the nutrient can be leached. Applying compost teas can sometimes lead to this problem, as the organisms introduced may put the whole soil population out of balance.

Soil organisms help to form humus which stores nutrients and holds water in the soil. Humus increases the flexibility of the soil to sustain plant growth into a hot, dry period and a creates a much reduced need for irrigation water. Just 2.2 pounds (1 kg) of humus can hold almost 9 pounds (4 kg) of water.

STEPS TO IMPROVING SOIL FERTILITY — OBSERVING YOUR CONDITIONS

The first step is to test your soil, pasture and water to understand what you have in the way of minerals in soil and plant material. At the point of collecting these items you should do a thorough physical examination of the soil, plants and animals, noticing how much air space or crumb structure is in the soil and how many worms are active and at what level they reside. How often do you take a spade, dig out a scoop from your pasture and have a look at what is going on underneath? Are there worms wriggling about, little hoppers, beetles or millipedes, and white fungal strands? Or does the soil look hard and lifeless? This is one of the initial things I do when I visit a farm, right after observing how the livestock and pasture look.

One thing to notice is whether the organic matter in the root zone is being consumed or is it gathering as a thatch layer? This will vary according to the season and moisture conditions.

Also look between the grass stems for worm castings. How many and how big they are should be noted.

In the pasture, take a look at what species of plants are present,

> ### *Observations of Your Farm*
> 1. Is the pasture soil healthy?
> 2. Are there worm casting present?
> 3. Is thatch building up in the pasture?
> 4. What pasture plants are eaten?
> 5. In what order do pasture plants get eaten?
> 6. Where are the drainage problems?
> 7. How bad are the slow draining areas?
> 8. How long does water sit on the surface?
> 9. What is the underlying rock?
> 10. Has the soil washed in or blown in?
> 11. What was on the land before it was farmed?
> 12. How long has the land been farmed?

what your animals are eating and in what order of preference they are being eaten?

Then look at the drainage. When it is wet, look at where and for how long the water lies on the surface before soaking in?

Knowing what sort of underlying rock your land sits upon and what sort of history it has had is also important information. How long has it been since the last ash shower, if you farm in an active volcanic region, or was the soil upon which you farm washed in or blown in by the wind?

What was on your land before it was farmed and for how long has it been farmed?

When all this information is assembled you can then decide what actions you should take to improve the performance of your land for what you wish to produce. This might be to apply minerals that are shown to be in deficit on your soil test. You might also consider applying a liquid fish, seaweed or biodynamic spray. The main point of difference between biodynamic and conventional farming is that all the nutrients should be biologically available, as opposed to being water-soluble with conventional methods. This means that a plant can choose to take up clean water when it needs to transpire and can

Earthworm castings are a superb indicator of a healthy pasture.

draw up nutrients when and as they are needed. The various measures you can take to activate your soil are discussed in upcoming chapters.

Many farms specialize in one or two enterprises which results in specific fertility needs and pasture requirements. For example, the dairy cow requires a different fodder from beef animals, sheep, goats or horses. Most of us look to minerals for answers to fertility problems, and many farmers take advice from the sales representatives of the various chemical fertilizer companies. From one aspect this is the cheapest advice but for some it can be the most expensive. How often does a fertilizer sales agent recommend something that his or her firm does not sell? Consequently little attention is paid to soil biology or the dynamics around life and growth.

Organic farmers generally focus on soil biology, but for the biodynamic practitioner, the dynamics and identity of the farm are the first considerations before soil biology, and biology comes before the minerals. From my perspective, all of those areas should be integrated together. In farming we are working with life and life processes that are interrelated. Focusing on only one thing can throw the rest out of balance.

When I approach a farmer I inquire about which area they understand best and ask them where they want to go. Then I consider their present farm situation and how the dynamics of energy, biology and minerals can be adjusted to help them work toward their goal.

A farmer's prime objective should be to get the fodder plants growing like weeds. My definition of a weed is a plant that self-propagates, grows luxuriantly, and for which one has not yet developed a market. To get our cultivated plants growing like weeds we often need to make some interventions. These interventions could be the addition of finely ground, mineral-rich rockdust, developing and encouraging the soil's aerobic biological life or managing the energy or dynamics of our farm environment consciously. To this end we might be working with composts, a manure heap, or an effluent to which special herbs, seaweed or biodynamic preparations might be added.

This is an extremely simplified look at one or two functions that occur in the soil. I have observed that when we have the whole organism of our farm or garden balanced in every respect, plants and animals are much better able to find the nutrition they need.

4

Soil Mineral Balance

I F your livestock are not as healthy as you would like them to be, maybe it's time to take a look at what they are eating. What are you using to grow the pasture? Whether you use soluble fertilizers or want to farm biologically, it's generally recognized that some amendments are needed, unless you have a very fertile soil. In soils that are deficient in major and trace elements, which includes most New Zealand soils, it would take a long time, if ever, to rectify these deficiencies without applying minerals. We are finding that our organic food needs to be more nutrient dense, and the same applies to food for your livestock.

There is now a huge range of products being sold to farmers from inorganic fertilizers to products that can be used on certified-organic farms. I am frequently asked, "How do I choose which products to use on my farm?" Choosing the right product requires an understanding of your farm situation, what it needs, and an understanding of what the product will do. The most important part of the situation is to know and appreciate what you already have in your soil. If you have been used to applying the prescribed amounts of N, P and K, working out what you need yourself may seem like a challenge but it's ultimately far more satisfying.

JUSTUS VON LIEBIG — THE FATHER OF MINERAL FERTILIZERS

The minerals used conventionally in soil amendments are but a few of the elements represented in the periodic table. About 150 years ago,

Justus von Liebig, a soil scientist noticed that a number of the mineral elements enhanced the growth of crops when they were present and detracted from the well-being and health of a crop when they were missing. Using a traditional method of growing food and managing our land that we would now describe as organic, von Liebig discovered that plants grew better when certain minerals were added to poor soils. But, he found that more fertile soils were usually not responsive to mineral supplementation. To improve plant uptake he devised a system of treating them with acid salts such as superphosphate and muriate of potash. Industry got hold of these ideas and when von Liebig came to the age of wisdom and decided that acid-based minerals were not the best way to supplement soil minerals, industry didn't want to let go of their bonanza. Acid-based fertilizers are still a major industry today.

By the early 20th century, nitrogen in several forms was being used as a growth stimulant. However, farmers were also beginning to notice differences in their crops. They had to buy new strains of seed more often as their homegrown seed was less viable and produced poorer crops. The flavors of food were no longer as the older folk remembered and meal satisfaction diminished. Regular and increasing use of water-soluble nutrients on the soil resulted in the natural soil fertility of our plants subtly being cut off from the plants. The results were manifold shortcomings in the health of the soil, plants, animals and humans.

CONVENTIONAL SOIL TESTS & AMENDMENTS FOCUS ON ONLY A FEW ELEMENTS

Even today many soil tests focus on only the levels of nitrogen, phosphorus and potassium in the soil. In New Zealand the first element to be supplemented was phosphorus in the form of superphosphate, that is phosphate rock treated with sulfuric acid. Later some serpentine was included in this to add a little magnesium to the soil. When this mix did not work so well any more, potassium was added to it. This element is commonly combined with chlorine and called muriate of potash. More recently, nitrogen fertilizer has become increasingly popular with farmers, orchardists and croppers. Concerns about the acidity of the soil have been addressed by adding lime.

On farms where a lot of these fertilizers have been applied over many years, such as in many parts of New Zealand, a knowledge of what is already in the soil and how this reacts with any new amendments is particularly important. Some farmed soils in New Zealand now contain 1,338-1,784 lbs/acre (1.5-2 tonnes/ha) of stored, but not easily accessible, phosphorus. It has formed insoluble compounds with aluminum, calcium and iron. A further problem that occurs with clay soils is that they often have so much potash bound into the clay that when lime is added, the lime releases potassium from the clay. The calcium becomes bound up in place of potassium and potash is released, often making an old problem worse. Too much potassium in pasture leads to metabolic problems such as bloat and staggers in livestock as it prevents them from getting sufficient calcium and magnesium.

Part of the problem is that the soil biology has become less active. All plants are dependent upon good soil biology for balanced mineral availability. The use of acidic fertilizers makes life much more difficult for aerobic soil life. With acidic fertilizer use the soil gets harder and the air that these soil organisms breathe diminishes even more. And so the downward spiral continues.

Since we are not getting an adequately mineralized food, many people go to the health food store or pharmacy to buy various mixes of dietary supplements. Humans and animals are best suited to taking minerals from the plant world. Plants obtain minerals from soil biology that dissolve them from the rock particles in the soil. The correct place to apply mineral dietary supplements is to add then to the soil as ground rock, not in salt form. The mineral balance needs to be such that a suitable environment is formed for the soil biology.

THE ALBRECHT MINERAL BALANCING SYSTEM

Those who have followed the work of Dr. William A. Albrecht, will see that a focus on only NPK and lime seems a rather simplistic view.

Albrecht was a university professor in the United States who observed in the 1930s where certain crops and pasture grew well and where they didn't — noting the grazing routes the wild buffalo had followed and the areas they had avoided. He took soil samples from each of these areas and compared them. From observation of the plants at each site, he and others who worked with him were then able to determine which effects each element had on certain plants. One of Albrecht's often quoted messages is, "If you would become a good farmer, study books and nature: if they differ throw the books away." He found that the relationship of one mineral to another is as important as having enough of each mineral. No mineral is an island unto itself — each reacts to all the others, just some more so than others.

I find that each element has its own life and character in the soil, plant and animal. One might say each element has a personality and a peculiar way of interacting with other elements as a person in a group or crowd might interact. Observation and study of the effects of these elements when used in homeopathy will help this understanding of the interactions, as their energy or dynamics is the vital aspect. Many of the elements are particularly important for the well-being of soil biology and the plant world. Weeds will often reflect what's going on both biologically and minerally. Still other elements are more vital to the well being of animals and humans.

Albrecht found that the concept of correcting high acidity — or low pH — with lime is too simplistic. Many minerals affect acidity/pH. For soil alkalinity Albrecht looked at not only calcium but magnesium, potassium, sodium, aluminum, hydrogen, and the trace elements iron, copper, zinc and cobalt. These elements are positive ions (cations) and, according to Albrecht, need to be in a particular ratio to enable plants to have ready access to each. If there is too much of one, another may become unavailable, thus causing a deficiency disease. An example of this might be if sodium is too high there is likely to be a deficiency of potassium showing up in plants. The effects of the various deficiencies impacts not only on plant health but also on the health of animals and of humans who eat the plants. Notice how popular dietary supplements are now!

On the other side of the ledger there are the negatively charged ions known as anions. They are either strongly or weakly acidic. The better known of these are sulfur, phosphorus, nitrate and chlorine. The aim when balancing minerals is to balance anions with cations to achieve a fairly neutral pH as well as to balance the cations with each other.

Mineral levels can be tested in the soil, the plant tissue, in an animal blood sample or in the liver. Sometimes samples taken from the soil, plants and animals differ considerably, showing different elements to be deficient in each place. Sometimes though there is a consistency among test results. I have observed that if there is a good biological activity in the soil the results are much more likely to be consistent. This is one of the things that I think biologically dynamic soils have going for them.

TRACE ELEMENTS

When doing a soil test I like to have a reading on the minor elements as well as the major elements, as many will either work synergistically or antagonistically with others. For example, if cobalt levels are too low your soil may have difficulty absorbing sufficient nitrogen from the atmosphere or if boron is too low, calcium in the lime may not be working as well as it should and so on. The main anion trace elements are boron, iodine, molybdenum and selenium. These elements are effective in the health of animals and humans and you will see a lot about them if you study homeopathy. Many of them react with or act as catalysts for other elements. Some of the minor elements are described as heavy metals and therefore have the capacity to be toxic when they are out of context or in isolation. While they are very important and needed in very small amounts, they should be treated with great respect. Boron, for example, is used in treating framing timber and as an ant poison. There are many more trace elements that are likely to contribute to plant and animal health. These trace elements can be supplied in a fresh, well-made liquid seaweed.

Trace element deficiencies also can reduce plant uptake of mineral elements. Primary elements such as calcium and phosphorus are activated by unstable trace elements such as boron and zinc. It is important to apply these trace elements accurately as you can easily apply too much, which becomes more of a problem than a deficiency. Once in the soil you can't take them out again. Trace elements work best through the soil biology. Fungi and bacteria consume the trace elements and then they become active in the life of the soil. Buffering the trace elements by chelating the minerals (coating the mineral particles in protein) is a very safe and effective method of application.

Trace elements are less deficient in the United Kingdom and Europe than in the United States, Australia and New Zealand. Also few British and European farmers have heard of the Albrecht mineral balancing system. Many farmers in the United States are familiar with it, and Brookside Laboratories does soil testing that follow Dr. Albercht's methods, as do other labs. Sixteen elements are commonly tested in a Brookside Laboratories soil test. When working out what amendments to apply based on this, the quantity of an element in relationship to other elements needs to be carefully calculated to enable each element to be accessed by the plant (and eventually by animals and humans). This balance is essential to our health. As you can see, there is a lot more to growing good grass than applying a bit more nitrogen.

PRACTICAL APPLICATIONS OF MINERAL BALANCING

In the introduction I wrote about the dairy farm where I grew up and said that the soil became deficient in phosphorus, affecting my health as well as that of the farm. The farm was situated on river flats with underlying marine clay. My parents did not want to apply mineral fertilizers as they were following organic and biodynamic principles. The natural soil fertility began to run out and the cows were not getting enough to eat. This was a hard lesson to learn firsthand. These days most farmers get soil tests done to check for deficiencies, but in those days you could only find out about what was happening in the soil by applying minerals to test patches of pasture and observing the results.

Phosphorus

Farmers have long been aware that most New Zealand soils are deficient in phosphorus and have applied superphosphate to correct this.

But now many farmers are observing that annual superphosphate topdressings are not providing the growth they used to. A closer look at what is going on in the soil is needed. One effect of the sulfur in superphosphate is that after the second or third dressing it starts to acidify the soil. Most farmers apply lime to correct acidic soils. The sulfur combines with the calcium from phosphate rock to make gypsum. If there is still some free sulfur left over it either combines with magnesium or remains as free sulfuric acid in the soil. Magnesium sulfate readily leaches, so magnesium also may then become deficient. Generally acidic soils are unable to store acids and they tend to leach over time. For example, nitrates frequently leach into waterways, resulting in fish deaths and algal blooms.

Lime

Applying lime has different effects on different soils, so it all depends on the type and condition of your soil and what you want to use it for. If you apply lime it tends to release the potassium that has been held by the soil. Lime is beneficial to clay soils because it flocculates it (opens up the soil particles). But a clay soil can contain a lot of potassium. If there is a lot of potassium from previous applications of potassium fertilizers, this can be a problem, particularly when growing pasture. The potassium reduces uptake of phosphorus, leading to shallow roots and grasses that can easily be pulled out by grazing cattle. Eating grass containing a lot of potassium leads to digestive problems in the cattle as it interferes with the rumen fermentation process. On the other hand if you apply lime to an orchard and the soil releases more potassium, this can be beneficial, as potassium is needed to grow good-sized fruit. For pastures, calcium could be applied as a sulfate, a small quantity at a time, to reduce the release of potassium. When lime is applied to sandy soils, potassium release is not generally an issue, but there is often a magnesium deficiency, so it may be better to apply dolomite.

Potassium

An excess of potassium in the soil is a particular problem when the soil gets wet and anaerobic, because the extra potassium may reduce to sodium. Wet soils are sticky, but they dry out rapidly when the rain stops, so there are not many times when pastures grow successfully under excessive sodium.

Potassium in the soil is readily taken up by plants. The plants then send sap to their periphery, encouraging rapid, watery growth. In contrast, sodium is hydroscopic, attracting moisture to it in the soil, and in the plant this causes wizened leaves and burn marks on leaf margins. In certain circumstances, such as pugged, wet, anaerobic soils, potassium may become reduced to sodium, and then the soil will not drain readily in the winter. This situation will also not let plants take up water in the summer, causing early drought stress. Most soils where potassium is in excess are compacted and roots have difficulty penetrating the soil to any depth. This can lead to pasture pulling, where livestock pull up clumps of grass.

Orchards and gardens require about double the potassium levels of pasture soils, i.e. ideally a ratio of one potassium to one phosphorus and three potassium to one sodium respectively. The importance of getting the correct relationships between your soil minerals in relation to crop production and soil types is vital for healthy plants and animals.

The yarrow plant (*Achillea millefolium*) can be an indicator when attention needs to be paid to potassium. This is the plant from which the biodynamic preparation 502 is made that helps to moderate potassium activity (see Chapter 9). In pasture, if potassium is in excess in relation to phosphorus, biodynamic preparation 501, also known as horn quartz or horn silica (as it is made from ground quartz, which contains silica, I will use the former name in the book), can be helpful (see Chapter 7) as it can promote the activity of phosphorus and also moderate potassium activity. Mineral fertilizers, serpentine or magnesium silicate have a similar effect.

High-pH Soils

In Australia and the United States, soils often have a high pH due to having a high magnesium content relative to the calcium and potassium levels. This can lead to a hard soil that is difficult for water to percolate into and quickly result in heavy rains sitting on the surface and becoming floods.

Sometimes soils become sodic with high concentrations of sodium, and are difficult to handle as sodium is hydroscopic, i.e. attracts moisture, so these soils do not drain well. When temperatures rise sodic soils do not let the plants have much moisture so early drought stress occurs.

Calcium

Calcium is the most important mineral nutrient in the soil after carbon. It is the main constituent of lime, where it combines with carbon and oxygen. Calcium is the element that can open tight soils, especially when it is combined with a little sulfur, as it does in gypsum. The requirements of different crops specify different levels of calcium from about 50 percent of the cation exchange as for blueberries, to perhaps 80 percent in the case of Brassicas on a heavy clay soil. Blueberries prefer an acidic soil in the region of 4.5 pH and grow well on peat soils. At the other extreme Brassicas do exceptionally well with high calcium and especially well if sulfur is there in good measure. Pasture requires an almost neutral soil from 6.2-6.8 pH. See Chapter 9 for ways that biodynamic preparations can be used to help balance calcium activity.

Calcium is the only mineral that can open up and expand soil. This is partly because it enables more growth of soil biological life. The other reason is that calcium is a larger ion than potassium and magnesium, so it pries apart the platelets of clay where it is stored, freeing the potassium.

Yet another reason for calcium's effect on the soil relates to the diamagnetic or paramagnetic qualities of different elements. Paramagnetic materials are attracted by external magnetic fields but do not become magnetic. In contrast, diamagnetic materials create a magnetic field in opposition to an externally applied magnetic field. The diamagnetic elements like calcium tend to flocculate or push particles apart while the paramagnetic ones tend to draw elements together. This shows once again the importance of having the correct balance of minerals for the intended use of the soil.

Humankind has transplanted European crops and cultures to many other parts of the world. For these crops to thrive we often need to change the mineral balance of the soil to be more like the native soil habitat of the plants.

Calcium Deficiency

When U.S. soil advisors Arden Andersen and Phil Wheeler visited New Zealand, they emphasized that it is the lack of calcium rather than the pH that is the problem in many soils. Most New Zealand soils are already deficient in calcium. Plants need calcium as well as phosphorus for growth. Much of the lime applied on New Zealand farms becomes unavailable for pasture uptake through being locked up as insoluble compounds. More soil biology activity, particularly fungal activity, is needed to hold the calcium in the soil and mobilize calcium to make it available to the pasture plants. We depend on this biological activity to make most of the soil minerals available for uptake when the plants need them. Most European soils have traditionally not been deficient in calcium, although they are becoming more so as farmers apply large quantities of nitrogen through effluent or fertilizers.

It is interesting to note that while humans and animals form solid bones from calcium, simpler organisms exude calcium outside themselves as a slimy coating or sometimes as a hard shell around them. Humans and animals with skeletons take calcium into the bones, while crustaceans like crabs and snails exude it into their shells. Calcium helps soft organisms, like many of our soil inhabitants, lubricate their passage through the soil. This is an important aspect to look for in worms — do they have slimy skins that glisten in the light; do small particles of soil adhere to them or are they clean? This is one indication of the calcium activity happening in the soil. Earthworms are important transformers, making inactive calcium into active calcium.

Calcium is used by soil biology to form calcium pectate. This is a digestive juice that digests minerals and also forms the lining of the soil cavities they live in. Calcium pectate helps with the formation of a good soil crumb structure by lining many very small channels called soil pores which enable the soil to hold more air. The ideal ratio for soil crumb and pore space is 50:50, with 50 percent of the pore space holding moisture and 50 percent holding air. Calcium pectate, as the living liquid form of calcium, and is most important for plant uptake and for combining with other elements such as sulfur, phosphorus, nitrate, selenium, molybdenum, boron and iodine. Calcium is the king of elements because of its soil-conditioning effect, as it moderates the availability of other minerals and is the main manager of soil acidity or alkalinity (soil pH). Calcium, after carbon, makes up the largest volume of active plant nutrient elements in the soil and is vital at all levels of life from soil substance to human well-being and everything in between.

I frequently used to hear a saying that "too much lime made fathers rich and sons poor." What is missing here to cause this situation? Is active carbon the missing element in this equation?

MINERAL INTERACTIONS IN A FARM SYSTEM

Minerals generally work in combination with each other. It is more important to get the balance between minerals right than to keep applying a mineral that was deficient. Calcium and phosphorus work together. If these two minerals are not in the right balance in the soil they may not be taken up into pasture or crop plants. On many farms and orchards that I have visited, leaf analysis shows a deficiency of either calcium or phosphorus in the plant. Sometimes there is plenty of an element in the soil, but it is not rising up into the plant. In many soils it appears that calcium uptake is the problem, but actually phosphorus uptake is a problem as well.

Temperature and moisture in the soil presents another variant as well. Moisture is needed for calcium and potassium to work freely, while warmth and light help the activity of phosphorus, magnesium and to a certain extent sulfur.

An understanding of how a whole system functions is required so you can observe where the process is not functioning at an optimum level and restore it. This requires knowledge of all the elements used by soil biology and how the various organisms feed on the mineral elements in the soil. There are 16-17 elements tested by Brookside Laboratories whereas soil organisms may use 30-40 elements. More and more it is being discovered that additional elements are needed (usually in small amounts) for plant growth. To farm better we need a thorough knowledge of all these elements and their interactions.

Various organic composts and liquid manures (such as seaweed and fish), and the biodynamic preparations help to encourage biological activity and the mobilization of mineral elements in the soil. I'll discuss these and the importance of balancing the calcium (growth forces) with the silica (energy forces) in Chapter 7. Soil biology is needed to digest and store soil minerals and make them available to plants. But the soil biology can only function properly if they can obtain all the minerals and carbon they need to grow and if the energy forces are sufficient and in balance.

A SUMMARY OF THE MAIN ELEMENTS FOUND IN SOILS THAT ARE IMPORTANT TO AGRICULTURE

Calcium is the most important mineral nutrient in the soil after carbon. It is the main constituent of lime where it combines with carbon and oxygen. Calcium is the element that can open tight soils especially when it is combined with a little sulfur, as it does in gypsum. The requirements of different crops specify different levels of calcium from about 50 percent of the cation exchange, as for blueberries, to perhaps 80 percent in the case of brassicas on a heavy clay soil.

Magnesium is found in dolomitic lime (New Zealand has 12 percent) and in serpentine rock (24 percent in New Zealand) where it is bound to a silicate. Generally magnesium should be about one seventh of the calcium value and from 10-15 percent of the cation exchange. High magnesium levels make a soil tighter. Magnesium is also the cornerstone of photosynthesis, and when there is not enough for the leaf, chlorosis, or yellow patches, in a green leaf may be found.

Sugars are formed as a result of photosynthesis. Sugars not only give leaves a more pleasant taste but also they are exuded from roots in turn feeding bacteria and fungi. Sugars have the highest protein levels of all soil organisms, so when they become the fodder of other organisms with less protein, nitrogen is excreted and bound into soil humus where it is accessible for plants as required. Living organisms breathe air, bringing all-important oxygen into the soil. The invigorated soil organisms can then release more phosphorus to the plant as well.

Potassium is an element that is vital to the fruiting process and acts to strengthen plant stems or trunks. It is the main constituent of wood ash (as potassium hydroxide), along with any charcoal that has not burned. If we still cooked our food over wood fires we would have adequate supplies of potassium for our plants without resorting to using potassium chloride or muriate of potash.

Chlorine is a trace element and is needed in small quantities for the soil, plants and animals, but not at the levels commonly used when potassium is applied. Another form is potassium sulfate (sulfate of potash), but once again do not oversupply sulfur. Biological activity in the soil generates a small amount of potash which can be almost enough if you are careful not to allow it to leach away. Three percent of the cation exchange is enough for pastures while 5 percent is adequate for fruit and vegetables.

Sodium is required in much smaller amounts. It is important for the health of animals and humans. It has the capacity to attract and hold moisture in the soil and plant. Too much in the soil causes the soil to be difficult to drain in the winter and to hold moisture from the plant in summer, causing early drought stress. Apples in dry climates are particularly sensitive to sodium. Sodium is most commonly found combined with chlorine, but in baking soda it is combined with carbonate. Baking soda is sometimes used as a remedy for fungal attacks in some plants, such as for black spot in apples. One percent of the cation exchange is the recommended level of this element, although 2 percent is also fine as long as the potassium level is at least double the sodium level.

Iron is needed to help plants achieve a dark green leaf thus iron assists photosynthesis. It also can lead to chlorosis if it is not present in sufficient quantity. Iron helps to carry oxygen in the blood of animals and humans. Iron levels above 50 ppm are considered adequate but higher amounts are often found. Watch out, though, in a low-pH soil iron can often tie up phosphorus.

Manganese is an element that is important for seed formation and should be present at about 25 ppm.

Zinc has a symbiotic relationship with phosphorus and is important for seed development, especially with nuts. In animals and humans it is important for a good autoimmune system. It is also important for male fertility. Eight ppm is the recommended level in soil.

Copper is important to assist iron in oxygenating tissue in animals. Copper is also important for female fertility. Copper deficiency in cattle can be seen as sway backs and a brownish tinge on otherwise black hair and rough coats. There may also be an issue with alopecia, or balding. Copper should be present in soil at about 5 ppm.

Boron is a minor element required at about 1 ppm in the soil where it is one of the catalysts for activating calcium. It helps to thrust sap out to the periphery of the plant so it is vital in fruiting plants — especially at flowering time. In animals and humans it is also connected to the management of calcium. Boron is the main ingredient in ant poison, so care should be taken with this element. In the mineral world it is found as ulexite and in the organic world boron is found in good compost.

Molybdenum is required in very small quantities (0.1 ppm) and is usually adequate when calcium is adequate. In my opinion it should not be added until calcium has been brought to the desired level. Molybdenum assists the nitrogen process and helps clover to thrive.

Cobalt is the base element of vitamin B12. It is important for nitrogen fixing in the soil and the ability to of animals and humans to digest protein. Cobalt is required in extremely small quantities in the soil, in the vicinity of 0.3 ppm.

Phosphorus is the most well-known of the agricultural anions or negatively charged elements. It has a relationship with zinc and should be ten times the value of zinc. Phosphorus is usually found in association with calcium at two parts of calcium to one of phosphorus.

Sulfur is the catalyst in agricultural chemistry. In my own New Zealand and elsewhere sulfur is leached by rain during periods of wet weather, especially in acidic soils. It combines readily with positive ions like calcium, magnesium and potassium, mobilizing them. Most soils need a little sulfur every year. It also moderates the availability of molybdenum. Phosphorus that is immobilized in the soil by calcium can be mobilized by sulfur removing some of the calcium, thus freeing phosphorus.

Selenium is important for livestock and human health. Selenium helps blood reach the capillary bed and is associated with vitamin E. It is required in such small quantities that it is not measurable in the soil.

Iodine is important in regulating warmth and relates to animals coming in season again after calving. Iodine can be found naturally in sea salt and seaweed, but in very small amounts.

5

Nitrogen and Oxygen in Plant Growth & Overcoming Leaching Problems

WE have long been told that nitrogen stimulates pasture growth. The form of nitrogen that is of interest to most pastoralists is nitrate (NO_3^-). Nitrate consists of one part nitrogen to three parts oxygen.

So, what is the active principle in the nitrogen fertilizing process? My understanding is that it is oxygen. The element that is active in all life processes is oxygen. Nitrogen is the transporter of oxygen through the plant. Oxygen has to be transported by another element through all life forms. For example, in animals, iron carries oxygen in hemoglobin, assisted by copper.

Air is 80 percent nitrogen and under average air pressure there is about 1,935 pounds/square yard (10.5 tonnes/square meter) of air, which means about 9.36 tons (8.5 tonnes) of nitrogen. So why would you buy nitrogen in a bag? It is far more cost effective to encourage the activity of soil bacteria species that convert atmospheric nitrogen into ammonium salts in the soil, then changing the ammonium into nitrites and nitrates that plants can use.

Oxygen is well recognized as the most active paramagnetic element (see Phil Callahan's book, *Paramagnetism,* 1995). A well oxygenated soil encourages a good root system. A good root system is vital to the well being of most of our cultivated plants.

To develop a well-oxygenated soil, active calcium is important. Active calcium opens or flocculates the soil, encouraging the soil biology to create pore space for air and moisture. This gives soils resilience against climate and weather extremes. Calcium is an important diamagnetic element, which is needed to stimulate the paramagnetic elements.

When calcium activity encourages biological activity, sugars are transformed to protein and the residual carbon from the sugars is transformed to humus. Humus contains good reserves of nitrogen, oxygen, potassium, calcium and phosphorus, all stored for plant use.

Applying water-soluble mineral nutrients has the opposite effect to the oxygenating process described above (i.e. smaller root systems and biology populations), therefore leading to more and more inputs being required to maintain good productivity.

Living organisms, including plants and animals, flourish when there is plenty of oxygen flowing through them. It is easy to recognize pasture that contains plenty of oxygen. It has a healthy, mid-green color, in contrast to yellow, sickly looking grass or the darker green grass with a bluish tinge which contains high levels of nitrate nitrogen.

EFFECTS OF APPLYING SOLUBLE NITROGEN FERTILIZERS

Some farmers are noticing that where nitrogen is applied out of a bag, more is needed within three to four months to prevent a fodder deficit. One dressing begets another and farmers find themselves on an expensive treadmill. How often have you heard this kind of conversation?

Salesman to farmer: "How ya doing? Your grass looks a bit yellow — about time you put on some more urea."

Farmer: "Seems I'm having to put on urea more and more frequently."

My question to farmers is, "Do you really want to be a put *more-on* farmer?"

Large nitrogen amendments lead to soil mineral imbalances and deficiencies, as well as a reduction in soil organism activity and deterioration in soil structure. Excessive nitrogen also results in mineral imbalances in grass foliage and an adverse effect on livestock health. All these effects are indications of inadequate oxygen in the soil. In many countries restrictions are being placed on the quantity of animals and fertilizers that can be put on an area of land to reduce the amount of nitrogen and other minerals leaching into groundwater and the environment. In New Zealand such restrictions are being put in place in the watersheds of Lake Taupo and Lake Rotorua. While visiting Switzerland an old farmer told me that there was, in his mind, a very clear link between the addition of nitrogen fertilizers and a sharp deterioration of water quality in the ponds and lakes.

So what happens when nitrogen is applied in ammonium form (NH_4^+)? If the soil is acidic the ammonium adheres well to the soil colloid, as ammonium is alkaline, but when it is oxidized to nitrate, oxygen is taken from the soil to combine with nitrogen, eventually leaving the soil with less oxygen and therefore with a lower paramagnetic quality. The fertilizer is fairly alkaline (i.e. relatively high pH) — as alkaline as urea — but when it is added to the soil and oxidizes to nitrate it becomes acidic. This happens when nitrates combine with the base elements hydrogen, calcium, potassium or magnesium. If it combines with hydrogen, nitric acid is formed, which is very corrosive. If it combines with calcium, magnesium and potassium, these elements are taken out of the soil and into plants, then they need to be replaced. If they are not replaced — which can happen — particularly in hay paddocks, grass eventually ceases to grow. The result that is noticed is less plant root growth that eventually leads to the plants being pulled out by cattle. The uprooted grass is then replaced by low-fertility flat weeds, or broadleaves, that do not make good milk-producing fodder. After several years pastures need to be resown to fill all the gaps in the sward. This is another expense that a well-managed farm does not have to make.

Pasture that has had urea applied is not fermented or digested by ruminant animals well. Not only do the animals receive poorer nutrition, but their manure is more acidic, containing more nitrogen which produces the dark green "dung patches" in pasture which animals avoid eating. I call this type of farming "gunpowder farming," because the fertilizers used are similar to gunpowder (potassium nitrate). They also have the effect of producing manure that explodes out of the unfortunate animals that have to eat the high-nitrogen pasture.

The effects of applying nitrogen depend on the condition of the soil and pasture where it is used. Many American and Australian soils are alkaline. If ammonium fertilizers are applied, the nitrogen is easily leached because it is alkaline, and the soil holds it less easily than acids. It is better to apply nitrogen as a nitrate. However applying this soluble form of nitrogen reduces the number and activity of soil organisms that "fix" nitrogen and reduces the uptake of trace elements into the pasture. Trace elements then have to be fed to the cattle as minerals, which are less effective and more expensive than providing them as a balanced component of grass. When Justus von Liebig saw these effects happening 150 years ago he changed his mind about water-soluble nutrients. It seems others do not learn so quickly.

In New Zealand, soils are acidic to slightly acidic, with pH levels of 4.5 to 6.8. In these soils alkaline ions, such as calcium and magnesium, become strongly attracted to the soil particles and the acid ions, such as nitrates and sulfates, leach away. With this type of soil it is preferable to add nitrogen in the form of ammonium compounds to avoid this leaching. However, as described above, this is not the *sustainable* answer. As bacterial action oxidizes ammonia to the nitrite form it is changed to nitrate (an acidic ion) that can leach or remove the calcium that was locked up with phosphate and release that as well.

To reduce problems associated with acidic soils, it is better to amend the soil to a near neutral pH around 6.5 to 6.8. At this level there will then be more alkaline ions for the acidic ions to attach to — so nitrates, sulfates and phosphates are sustained longer in the soil and are less likely to be leached away. In a soil with a more balanced pH, the soil is generally open with a much greater biological activity. Adding calcium to the soil has the effect of opening up the soil, enabling aerobic soil organisms to thrive, as described earlier. Soil organisms create more pore spaces, allowing more air to circulate, and become part of the breathing process of the soil. Air is known to be 80 percent nitrogen and almost 20 percent oxygen. As I mentioned previously, it is cheaper and more effective to enable nitrogen-fixing organisms to collect nitrogen from the air rather than apply your nitrogen from a bag. Also, as soil pH becomes more neutral, especially higher than pH 6.2, clover nodules become more active, fixing more nitrogen from the air.

OVERCOMING LEACHING PROBLEMS

Minerals are frequently leaching from our soils causing concerns about contamination of the groundwater, as well as lake turbidity and weed growth. This is especially true in the New Zealand tourist icon lakes: Taupo, Rotorua and Rotoiti. When nitrogen leaches into water as nitrate it poisons fish, all other non-plant life then proceeds to diminish, while aquatic plant life flourishes. Nitrate is well known for blocking oxygen transport in fish and other water-dwelling animals as well as in humans and cattle — sometimes even causing cattle death from the nitrate poisoning. Nitrate also upsets the normal function of the rumen in ruminant animals, resulting in methane emissions and health problems from mineral imbalances. Farmers see a conflict situation here. Nitrate is the element of greatest concern reaching the lakes, but it is seen to be the main driver of added pasture production. Farmers believe that nitrates are needed to keep their incomes ahead of their costs. Let's examine this statement based on the relationship of nitrates to the other elements in the soil and see how they interact with the soil itself. If farmers were financially liable for the nitrates and phosphates lost from their land they would find their current practices less profitable. I know a number of farmers where their net profit is improved by farming biologically and switching to meet the requirements of organic certification.

What practical steps can we take to maintain plant growth and improve production without increasing the pollution load carried by our drainage water? Surely if we have to purchase inputs for our land we would want to retain as much as possible to stay and work on our land.

The first step is to ensure that there is sufficient calcium in the soil. Calcium raises the pH to a level that favors growth of beneficial soil organisms. It also opens up soils, creating air spaces where soil organisms can grow. In addition, calcium is an important nutrient for soil organisms. These organisms include the bacteria contained in legume nodules that fix nitrogen. When soil organisms become active and multiply they build nitrogen, oxygen, carbon and minerals into their body proteins. When these elements are in soil organism bodies they cannot be leached out of the soil. These organisms also help to make humus, which holds minerals in a stable form. So maintaining a large, active soil organism population ensures that minerals are not leached, but held in the soil and made available only to plants.

For many farms, providing calcium to the soil is not as simple as applying lime. As discussed in Chapter 4, calcium needs to be in the right relationship to several other minerals such as magnesium, potassium, sodium, copper, zinc and cobalt.

The next step is to combine mineral amendments with carbon before adding them to the soil. If you apply calcium, phosphorus and other minerals to soil when you have a large, active soil organism population, the minerals can kill soil organisms by dehydration or localized excessive alkalinity. Combining the lime or other fertilizer with carbon prevents these problems, and the soil organisms are able to assimilate the lime. The form of carbon often used for this purpose is leonardite, which is a form of humic acid. It is a black powder (like coal dust) that has been mined from very old carbon deposits. Any old coal dust can't be used as there may be contamination by heavy metals.

Humic acid is a major component of humus. The more commonly known form of humus is worm castings or organic material that has been digested by soil organisms. For the soil, adding a little at a time and more often is better — once the initial top dressings have been made.

Building the humus content of your soil is another important way to avoid the leaching of plant nutrients. When they are incorporated into humus they cannot be washed out, as humus is a very stable substance.

Several fertilizer producers now sell fertilizers that have been stabilized with carbon. Some add humic acid, others put fertilizers such as reactive phosphate rock, dolomite and lime through a composting process. The phosphorus, magnesium and lime in these products are readily available both to soil organisms and to plants as a result of a biological process.

I have made compost from reactive phosphate rock, dolomite, quarry dust, and trace elements. At the beginning the mineral content was 25 percent of the total volume, the other 75 percent was organic matter from plants and animals. After four months and four turns, the heap was reduced to twice the volume of the original minerals, and there was no visible evidence of any rockdust particles, some of which had been up to ¼ inch (7mm) in diameter. All of these minerals must have been consumed by organisms. Two weeks after my application of it to the pasture, grass growth appeared to be double the previous rate — a growth rate that was maintained for several subsequent seasons, from just one treatment.

It is also preferable to add carbon or protein to minor or trace elements before applying them to the pasture. Minor or trace elements may be chelated or wrapped in protein to buffer the soil organisms against extreme cases of localized acidity and to reduce the likelihood of leaching.

Once the soil organism population and humus content of your soil have been built up, nitrogen fertilizer can be applied with less danger of leaching as it also becomes part of the soil organism cycle. Many farmers find they no longer need the nitrogen because the population of nitrifying bacteria in the soil has built up. These bacteria fix nitrogen from the air and subsequently worms incorporate it into their castings.

Near our home there is a small cheese factory on a 50-cow dairy farm. I complimented the cheese maker on the quality and flavor of his products, adding that if he was using organic milk it would be even better. His response was, "That is fine so long as I can still use nitrogen." My response was, "Yes, certainly, but after a while you might find you do not need it anymore." We were then contracted to take a soil sample for a laboratory test and to make a recommendation. In due course we handed over the recommendations relative to his two different soil types and suggested that he not apply it all at once. It was applied in two dressings over a two-year time period. We were then asked to return and repeat the sampling. The first thing we noted was the change in the pasture both in quality and quantity and the weeds that had been a concern were no longer evident. Although the soil was very wet, with surface puddles in places, clover was flourishing. When I put a spade into the soil under water air bubbles came up. This showed that there was a lot of air in the soil in spite of it being covered with water. There must have been a lot of soil organisms flourishing to produce the air bubbles and the good pasture growth.

The lab report showed that there were only minor adjustments needed to be made to some minerals to have the relationships suggested by Dr. Albrecht. No further nitrogen fertilizer was needed, more and better grass was being grown, and the cows were healthier. In due course the dairy farm did obtain its organic certification.

In conclusion, plant nutrients in the soil are much less likely to leach if they are incorporated into the living soil along with carbon. Rudolf Steiner, the founder of the biodynamic method, discussing soil fertility with a group of farmers, said, "Remain within the sphere of life." When there are strong populations of soil organisms cycling nutrients, they keep these nutrients within the sphere of life. In this way productive output can be maintained while reducing the leaching of nitrates, sulfates and phosphates to the surface and groundwater, losing nitrous oxide and methane to the air. So you *can* have your cake and eat it too, in many cases with an even better net profit than you had before. And for certain the cake tastes better with healthy soil.

6

Biodynamic Systems for New World Farmers

SUCCESSFUL biological farmers grow large populations of active soil biology to feed their crops and pastures. Compost teas can be used to achieve this, but if soil conditions are not suitable, the organisms do not live long. The greater the range, or diversity, of the organisms, the more resilient and adaptable the soil is to changing conditions such as climate extremes. To achieve this good mix of biology, farmers need to create the right environment in the soil by making the best possible use of resources that are available on the farm.

The principles of biodynamics will provide some extra methods that can be used in biological and organic systems to enhance biological activity, increase flexibility, and grow high-quality products. Biodynamic farmers and growers find there are many benefits including that they need to use less irrigation water. Some have found they can even manage with 25 percent of the water used by other growers. At Nick Mills' biodynamic vineyard in a very dry climate located at Wanaka, New Zealand, the vines are not irrigated and produce very high-quality wine.

The system of farming we now call biodynamics was developed from a set of recommendations by Rudolf Steiner, an Austrian scientist/philosopher. Farmers in Germany had asked him how they could halt a decline in grain quality that they had noticed. They kept putting considerable pressure on him to come and talk to them. At this point Steiner already had a reputation for providing new insights to assist many other fields, including education and medical science. The Germans were already good farmers, farming good soil

Vines grow without irrigation at Rippon Vineyard and Winery in New Zealand, farmed biodynamically for many years by the Mills family.

in Europe, but they wanted to farm better. Steiner finally agreed to speak to the group and gave a series of lectures to the farmers in 1924. These lectures have been translated and are available as a book simply titled, *Agriculture Course*. The current biodynamic farming system has developed from these lectures and is practiced around the world.

The word biodynamics is short for "biologically dynamic" which is really what a biological farming system is about, aiming for a fertile, sustainable, productive farm. The dynamic part of the title refers to the management of energy. Some farmers have avoided biodynamics because they think it is too complicated or mystical, but really it provides farmers with practical tools which can be used to the extent that time and resources allow. Steiner was adamant that, "It must pay." He believed that if you are running a business you cannot afford to not be businesslike.

The important thing to realize is that these biodynamic practices were intended to supplement good farming practices and mainly to enhance quality rather than the quantity of production. They were introduced when farms were smaller and where larger farms had plenty of labor. It is more of a challenge to apply these principles and practices to larger, less fertile farms in New World countries. In Australia some farms are so large that even aerial spraying is too costly.

APPLYING BIODYNAMICS TO LARGE FARMS IN THE NEW WORLD

In much of New Zealand, Australia and North America there has not been a long tradition of farming and many of the soils are basically of low fertility and deficient in many minerals. European crops and farming systems have been introduced that do not compete well with the native plants that are adapted to these conditions — that is unless we first adjust the soil mineral balance. Applying biodynamic preparations to these soils helps to improve their fertility, but it takes many years before it will work well. Biodynamic preparations work best on farms where organic and/or biological systems have been established.

An additional feature of New World farms is that they are generally specialized, with one or just a few enterprises. Many are large-scale pastoral farms or orchards aiming to supply one or a small number of specific products for export, in contrast to smaller, mixed farms that mainly supply numerous products to local markets in Europe.

The ideal biodynamic farm has the right mix of cattle, pigs, poultry, sheep, horses and various crops that bring a balanced condition to the whole farm. Steiner recommended that if you have the right numbers and mix of different animals, their manures will enable the farm to be run productively without needing any outside inputs. Each of the animal manures has its own unique quality, making self-sufficiency much more possible. A specialized farm cannot attain this balance. As a result, many New World farms tend to be unbalanced with mineral deficiencies showing up. We therefore need to address this imbalance with outside inputs as well as biodynamic practices.

Most large-scale New World farms employ few people. They often do not have the time to make and apply biodynamic preparations in the traditional way. These farmers therefore need to be innovative to be successful with biodynamics. Rudolf Steiner repeatedly said in his lectures that he was giving out some ideas that farmers would need to develop — they were not intended as recipes to follow step-by-step. A farmer needs to adapt these ideas to suit his or her particular circumstances.

In most New World countries the climate is warmer than in Europe, enabling grass to grow for much of the year, so farming practices are different. In Europe the biodynamic preparations are mainly applied to regulate and enhance seasonal plant growth. Cattle are grazed on pasture when it grows in spring and summer and mainly fed hay and silage in winter months. In New Zealand, dairy cattle graze pasture all year, with only a little supplementation with hay and silage when drought or cold weather reduce pasture growth. The biodynamic preparations can therefore be used strategically to help optimize pasture growth and quality all year round.

Consultants, such as your author, strive to help farmers apply the principles of biodynamics and find practices that they are able to fit into the routines of their farming systems. When I advise a farmer or orchardist, I don't try to "sell" biodynamics or any particular inputs. I always start with a discussion of where they are at right now: their particular circumstances, goals and what they are comfortable with doing. A farmer who has been farming with nitrogen and other soluble fertilizers for many years and who may have a large mortgage is not in a position to make drastic changes. She or he needs to first understand that improving the biological activity in the soil is what will make a difference, and then have a program in place to gradually bring this about over a number of years. This program may include adding minerals that are deficient, preferably in composted or chelated form, to provide biological organisms and the nutrition they need to flourish. The biodynamic preparation 500 and other products that stimulate biological life, such as seaweed, fish extract and compost teas, are also helpful.

A farmer who has been farming organically for many years also might have a mineral imbalance that is preventing his farm from producing as well as it should, and this imbalance may be behind animal issues, crop health or weed problems. Many farmers ask me whether they should use a particular product on their farm. There is now available a bewildering array of products for organic farmers. I usually recommend that farmers try a little on part of a paddock to see if it makes a difference, as no matter how good a product is it is only helpful if your property needs it. If your refrigerator is already full of butter you don't need to buy more butter — however good the butter is. I prefer to help farmers understand what their soil needs and what kind of products can assist to build it better.

So, in this book I am discussing how a farmer can build up the soil, animal and crop health and the productivity of the farm. In doing so, we draw from a wide range of available tools, and selecting those most suitable for particular farm conditions and circumstances. Success depends upon using the right mix of all these tools. I focus particularly on biodynamics as this has been my passion for many years, but I often point out to my clients that biodynamics is really the icing on the cake — and sometimes it is necessary to first build the cake.

The foundation of any farm is the geological structure. Farms perform quite differently depending on what lies deep below, whether on granite, pumice, loess, sedimentary rock, sand, silt, marl or clay. Then there is the general soil type — whether gravel, sand, silt, limestone, ash, peat, clay or loam. Also of issue is whether it is well or poorly mineralized and whether there is a good or poor population of soil biology. Other important factors include the climate and aspect to sun, rain and wind. Onto all this we build our personality and management style, our preferences for plant and animal types and the general management style we wish to follow. The farm is complex, interconnected and is best analyzed as a whole entity.

Biodynamics

A SHORT, PRACTICAL INTRODUCTION

Ehrenfried E. Pfeiffer

The biodynamic farming and gardening method has grown and developed, since 1922, on a foundation of advice and instruction given by the late Rudolf Steiner, a philosopher known for his world view called anthroposophy (wisdom of man).

The name "biodynamic" refers to "working with the energies which create and maintain life." This is what was meant in the name given it by the first group of farmers inspired by Rudolf Steiner to put the new method to field use as well as practical tests. The term derives from two Greek words *bios* (life) and *dynamis* (energy). The use of the word "method" indicates that one is not dealing merely with the production of another fertilizer, organic though it is, but rather that certain principles are involved which in their practical application secure a healthy soil and healthy plants which in turn produce healthful food for man and healthy feed for animals.

WHAT ARE THE BIODYNAMIC PRINCIPLES?

1. To restore to the soil the organic matter which it needs so badly in order to hold its fertility in the form of the very best humus.

2. To restore to the soil a balanced system of functions. This requires our looking at the soil not only as a mixture or aggregation of chemicals, mineral or organic, but as a living system. We speak therefore of a living soil, including here both its micro-

life and the conditions under which this micro-life can be fully established, maintained and increased.

3. While the biodynamic method does not deny the role, and importance, of the mineral constituents of the soil — especially the so-called fertilizer elements and compounds that include nitrogen, phosphate, potash, lime, magnesium, and the trace minerals — it sponsors the most skillful use of organic matter as the basic factor for soil life. (It is of interest that the importance of the finer elements, the trace minerals, for health and normal growth was actually pointed out by Rudolf Steiner as early as 1924.)

However, the biodynamic method is more than just another organic method. It stands for a truly scientific way of producing humus. Not merely the application of "nothing but" organic matter in a more or less decomposed form is intended, but the use of the completely digested form of crude organic matter known as *stabilized, stable* or *lasting humus*. In this aim the method differs from what is commonly called "organic" farming. In the latter, any collection of any organic matter is apt to be called compost. In the B.D. method the organic material to be used as a basis for compost is transformed either by means of the so-called biodynamic preparations, or recently in the U.S.A. by means of the B.D. compost starter (Dr. Pfeiffer's formula).

It should not be forgotten that at the time of the creation of the method, during the years 1922-24, and afterwards during the years of experimental and empirical trials (from 1924 to about 1930), agriculture was dominated by the agricultural chemical concept based on Justus von Liebig's research with regard to the major mineral fertilizer elements. A one-sided situation had developed. Nitrogen, phosphate, potash, lime were considered the only important fertilizers and the trace minerals were ignored. Barnyard manure was looked down upon as an unimportant factor, frequently as a nuisance which had to be disposed of one way or another.

A fundamental change in the estimation of the value of manure and compost has taken place since 1930, increasingly since 1940, land of the trace elements since 1950. This has gone so far that manure and compost have now been restored to their proper, all-important position in modern agriculture, even in the orthodox school.

4. Since in the biodynamic method we speak not only of fertilizer but of the skillful application of all the factors contributing to soil life and health, it is necessary to understand that life is more than just chemicals (inorganic and organic). Life and health depend on the interaction of matter and energies. A plant grows under the influence of light and warmth, that is, *energies,* and transforms these energies into chemically active energies by way of photosynthesis. A plant consists not only of mineral elements, i.e. inorganic matter — these elements make up only 2-5 percent (in a few wild plants and weeds up to 10 percent) of its substance — but also of organic matter such as protein, carbohydrates, cellulose, starch, all of which derive from the air (carbon dioxide, nitrogen, oxygen) and make up the major part of the plant mass aside from water, namely 15-20 percent. The greater part of the plant mass, some 70 percent or more, consists of water.

5. The interaction of the substantial components and energy factors forms a balanced system. Only when a soil is balanced can a healthy, i.e. well balanced, plant grow and transmit both substance and energy as food. We live not only from substance (matter), we also need energies (life-giving land life-maintaining). It is the aim of the biodynamic method, or concept, to establish a system that brings into balance *all* factors which maintain life.

6. Were we to concentrate only on nitrogen, phosphate and potash, we would neglect the important role of biocatalysts (for

instance the trace minerals), of enzymes, growth hormones and other transmitters of energy reactions. As noted previously, already in 1924 Rudolf Steiner had called our attention to the important role of the finer elements (now called trace elements), in connection with health and proper physiological functioning. Today this is common knowledge. Enzymes and growth substances are likewise important. In the biodynamic way of treating manure and composts the knowledge of enzymatic, hormone and other factors is included.

7. In order to restore and maintain the balance in a soil a proper crop rotation is necessary. Soil-exhausting crops with heavy demands on fertilizing elements should alternate with neutral or even fertility-restoring crops — on the farm as well as in the garden, and even in the forest.

A soil which has been put to maximum effort, producing corn, potatoes, tomatoes, peppers and cabbage, for instance (all of them greedy crops), should have a rest period with restoring crops such as all the legumes. Temporary cover with grass and clover pastures helps to improve the humus and nitrogen situation. Exhausting crops and arable cultivation consume humus. The soil must be given time to build it up again.

The biodynamic method therefore has emphasized the importance of crop rotation from its very beginnings. Cover crops and green manuring also play an important role in it.

8. The entire environment of a farm or garden is of importance too. It is obvious that polluted air loaded with the breakdown products of industrial and city combustion, gasoline and oil fumes, sulfuric acid, can be detrimental to plant growth. It is less obvious that many other environmental factors also affect the functioning of a biological system. Deforested hillsides are exposed to erosion. The water balance may be destroyed in such cases. The ground water level has dropped. The results of manmade deserts are only too well known. To

restore the most beneficial environmental conditions (forests, wind protection, water regulation), has been an important aim of the biodynamic method from its earliest years. Had the method been accepted before 1930, it can be truly said that no soil conservation agencies would have been needed later on, in 1935 and the following years.

9. The soil is not only a chemical, mineral-organic system, but it also has a physical structure. The maintenance of a crumbly, friable, deep, well-aerated structure is an absolute must if one wants to have a fertile soil. All factors which lead to structural disintegration of the soil (for instance plowing of a too-wet soil, and especially the deep plowing of wet clay soils) and what causes the formation of separating layers (hardpan), are things that have to be known. The biodynamic method is very specific about the proper cultivation of the soil in order to avoid structural damage. Many a farmer, even among the organic farmers, has defeated his aim by ruining the soil structure through unskillful cultivation.

Ehrenfried E. Pfeiffer was was a German scientist, soil scientist, leading advocate of biodynamic agriculture, anthroposophist and disciple of Rudolf Steiner. He was a prolific author, speaker, and experimenter.

7
Calcium, Silica & BD Prep 500 and 501

THE management style that is particular to this book is one that manages energy — the "dynamics" of biodynamics, the energy management of biology. Biodynamic methods are only useful if you understand what they are doing and can use them appropriately.

THE CALCIUM & SILICA PROCESSES

When Rudolf Steiner talked to farmers about improving the quality of their crops and animals, he talked about the opposite effects of the "calcium and silica processes." The calcium process affects the earthly energies that promote plant growth, while the silica process affects flowering, seeding and product quality. These two processes — what they do and what conditions favor them — are described in lecture one of Steiner's *Agriculture Course*.

We are used to thinking of calcium as a solid mineral, as in lime, that you can spread on the land to raise the pH. But when we look at the soil, plants and animals, a mineral is not generally static in one form, it is continually changing from one compound to another, reacting with other elements, dissolving in water, and moving in and out of cells. Generally a particular mineral has a typical way of working, and produces predictable effects on the whole organism. We can think of this as its process or activity and see its effect in the way plants and all living organisms grow.

Calcium can be seen in a fluid form in the secretions of slugs, snails and earthworms. One of the easiest tests for calcium activity is to observe an earthworm taken from the soil. How does it glisten in the light? Are there any crumbs or particles of soil stuck to it? The more it glistens and the cleaner it is, the better the calcium is working. Calcium is very important to soil biology, and soil biology is important to have a good supply of many elements move from the soil to plants. Having calcium active in the soil helps soil flocculation and helps with the assimilation of organic matter into humus.

If a plant is growing where there is insufficient calcium process it tends to have long, thin, twining stems, producing infertile flowers and have very little product. On the other hand, if there is insufficient silica process, the plant will have a pyramidal form, rather like a cactus (being thicker at the base), and producing no seed or grain.

Steiner said that these mineral processes are affected by energies coming from the planets. The planets that are farther away from the sun than the earth — Mars, Jupiter and Saturn — affect the silica process, while Mercury, Venus and the moon, the nearer planets, affect the calcium process. Generally people do not think of the planets as having much effect on us here on the earth, but in fact they have a large effect. Think of the moon's effect on tides, weather, fishing seasons, etc. Interestingly plants are more directly affected by the planets than animals.

The calcium process brings moon energy, which is greatest during the winter months. If you observe the positions of the sun and the moon, you may notice that the full moon is at a higher altitude in the sky during the winter months, when the sun is at a lower altitude. The successive positions of the full moon during winter months follow the same course as the sun follows in summer. As a result, there are stronger energies from moon-reflected sunlight in the winter compared to summer, and stronger direct sunlight in summer.

These processes are happening all the time above and below our soils. Calcium is most active in the moist times of the winter and least active in the summer when it is hot and dry. The silica process, which also stimulates phosphorus and magnesium activities, is supported by warmth. In the earth's silica process, light is stored by silica-based rocks, stones and sand. The light provides energy for plant roots and soil organisms to take up nutrients. The capacity of a soil to provide light energy to plants therefore depends on whether there are light-storing rocks underneath. It also depends on whether there is clay in the soil to transmit the light up to plants. A predominantly clay soil tends to reflect more light, so it stores less. The effectiveness and balance of the calcium and silica processes that naturally occur can therefore vary considerably depending on the type of soil and underlying rock where your farm is situated.

PREPARATIONS 500 & 501

Rudolf Steiner recommended that farmers make special preparations to use to enliven the soil and to enhance and regulate the calcium and silica energy processes. The biodynamic horn manure preparation, which regulates the calcium process, is being applied by increasing numbers of farmers to their land. It helps to increase and activate aerobic soil biology, resulting in more open soil, better-rooted plants, and more plant resilience to a range of conditions. Some farmers who have used the horn manure for several years have found their topsoil depth has noticeably increased. They have also found better soil structure, tilth, and a greater capacity to absorb water and hold it into a dry period. In practical terms, this means a considerable reduction in irrigation costs and an increase in production.

The second preparation, horn quartz, is applied to plants, to regulate the silica process and enhance the effects of summer sunlight.

These preparations were also called preparation 500 and 501 respectively. Steiner's numbering system started at number 500 because the lower numbers had already been allocated to medical preparations. Several other biodynamic preparations are recommended, and are described in Chapter 9. All the preparations are made from simple materials that usually come easily to hand (or at least they did in 1924 when Steiner developed them). Today farming also has to deal with enthusiastic regulation makers who now deem many of the materials used to be hazardous to human health. These regulations make it harder to obtain materials needed for making preparations, although ideally they should all be grown on your farm.

The author fills cows horns with manure to be buried, yielding preparation 500 on Windriver Farm, Manawatu, New Zealand.

The preparation 500 is made by burying cow horns filled with cow manure in the soil over the winter months. To make preparation 501 (horn quartz), the horns are filled with ground, moistened quartz crystals and buried in soil during the summer months. The horns reflect and concentrate the light energies entering the soil into the contents of the horn. It is these energies that are important in the preparations that are subsequently applied to the farm.

Stirring preparation 500 can be a community activity.

USING BD PREPARATIONS 500 & 501 TO BALANCE PLANT GROWTH

Farmers generally apply preparation 500 in the spring and/or autumn and many do not use preparation 501 at all. I have found that these preparations are most effective when they are used at appropriate times to balance growth and light energies. To do this you need an understanding of how they work and the energies involved.

The BD preparations 500 and 501 can be used to counteract extremes of either the calcium or silica process, such as very damp and cool, or very hot and dry conditions. You can get a feel for when it is appropriate to use these preparations by observing the different kinds of light present in winter and summer. During the winter months, when preparation 500 is being made in a cow's horn underground, the sunlight is less intense, and there is also more moonlight (reflected sunlight) as the full moon is up for as long as the sun is in the summer. On the other hand, preparation 501 is made during the summer months when the summer sunlight is more intense. So this preparation contains the energy of summer sunshine, different from preparation 500 which contains winter sunshine energy.

While this is a simplistic view I feel that it helps people to choose the best times to use each of these preparations. For example, preparation 501 is helpful in cool, moist conditions when there is a lack of summer sunshine. This could be used if the plant is too soft and wet, sucking insects are bothering plants, or the plant's sap is too bitter due to excessive nitrates in the leaves or fruits. I have found that one spraying of 501 on pasture when the growth is soft and lush generally doubles the brix (soluble solids) reading. This has helpful consequences in the milk vat and shows as an increase in the dairy check each month. Once the weather becomes hot and dry this spray is no longer useful except for sweetening and drying hay and silage and ripening fruit.

Preparation 500 can be used when one needs to tilt the balance a little more toward the qualities of winter growth. The winter sun is active when the soil's digestive process is at its peak. Fine root hairs grow, getting the plant ready for next season's growth, soil biology grows and develops and the soil often deepens as a result. The deeper soil enables it to hold more living carbon, and more calcium, magnesium, potassium, etc. Steiner speaks of how moisture enhances the calcium process and warmth enhances the silica process. So if there is excessive moisture about, or no moisture, applying preparation 500 will not make much difference — the most productive time to apply it is when there is a little rain during a time when the soil is drying out.

Biodynamic preparation 500 is being spread by hand.

To ready preparation 500 for application, the horn manure is diluted in water, and stirred for one hour, then sprayed on the soil or pasture in the late afternoon or evening. Vigorous stirring in alternating directions has been shown to supersaturate the oxygen and bring rhythm into the liquid. Measurements of oxygen up to 12 parts per million are common when liquids are stirred vigorously in alternating directions. This results in rapid multiplication of aerobic organisms. Stirring also brings rhythm to the liquid, as all life needs rhythm.

When dealing with a living organism such as a farm, you should work with living substances and living processes as far as it is possible.

Preparation 500 should primarily be used in the spring, after it has been dug up, to carry the calcium process into the summer. I have noticed, in New Zealand, that everything suddenly starts drying out around the time when the sun goes into the constellation of Libra (around 1 November) — you can see the change from the calcium process to a silica process in the grasses and other plants in which growth slows down and they start to go to flower and seed. In the Northern hemisphere this time is when the sun enters the background of Aries, Gemini and Leo (late March to late July). For dairy farmers, who need the grass to keep growing in a leafy form, this is the ideal time to spray on preparation 500, if there is an imminent rain

Biodynamic preparation 501 is being sprayed on this dairy farm paddock.

shower. Stirred preparation 500 needs to be applied to the soil with enough moisture to germinate seeds. It is best applied in the evening when there is a condensing process in the atmosphere, to help carry the 500 into the soil where it works best. If there is no rain, there is no point in stirring 500 and applying it. In very dry areas, it is better to apply it homeopathically or via radionics, two specialized methods. Homeopathic application will discussed, but radionics is beyond the scope of this book.

Preparation 501 should mainly be used in the autumn after it is dug up, to extend the summer warmth and light into the darker period of the year. This applies particularly to pastures used for grazing animals. Preparation 501 is also stirred for one hour in water and then applied as a field spray to enhance the silica process — to balance the lack of light or strong, watery growth. A further activity of 501 is to help vertical root growth therefore helping drought resistance if applied in the early spring as the water table is dropping. This process is further enhanced when the moon has the constellations of Taurus, Virgo or Capricorn as a background.

Some farmers who use the preparations put preparation 500 on once in the autumn and preparation 501 once in the spring. This is not so helpful as the first preparation has stopped working by the time the second one is applied. Preparation 500, or any preparation for that matter, if applied alone would exaggerate the natural processes rather than balance them. In fact applying one preparation alone may well result in less production and production of a poorer quality — which may have a negative effect. Preparation 501 can burn some crops if applied in the spring and if it is more than three months after the last preparation 500 application. This is because before you apply preparation 501 there needs to be sufficient upward growth energy, which is stimulated by preparation 500, to balance the effect of the extra light brought on by the preparation 501. As the effect of preparation 500 wears off after about three months, if preparation 501 is put on in the spring about six months after the preparation 500, it will be as though no preparation 500 had been put at all. Preparation 501 acts in isolation to shrivel and burn the plants, particularly if the weather is warm and dry. Reduced subsequent growth may also be experienced, so *always* be sure that preparation 500 (or a compost or liquid manure made with compost preparations) has been used in the last two to three months before using preparation 501. Failure to observe this could lessen future plant growth.

To demonstrate how powerful these preparations are I often cite my experience with my lawn in Paeroa, New Zealand. The first two times I mowed it, in October and November (our seasons are opposite of North America), I followed up with a spray of preparation 501 in its homeopathic form. For almost five years, one mowing per month was adequate to keep the lawn in good trim and in late summer it stretched out to two or three months. This would not be a good look on a dairy farm. The lesson here is to always ensure preparation 500 is active before using preparation 501.

Soil tests done on my lawn six months later showed calcium suppressed and, using the Mehlich 3[1] test, phosphorus elevated in rela-

---

[1] The Bray 2 test indicates soil reserves of phosphorus, in comparison to the Mehlich 3 test which is a softer extraction, giving a better idea of the level of phosphorus available to the plant. In New Zealand the Resin P. test has a similar score to the Mehlich 3 test. For example, often with a soil test where the Mehlich 3 test shows 55 ppm, the Bray 2 test will show 120 ppm.

tionship to calcium. A Bray 2 extraction method used to test phosphorus in this lawn area where there had been no or very little historical application of phosphorus fertilizers also showed it was elevated in relation to calcium. Years later, Brookside Laboratories showed a Bray 2 phosphorus test result with a significantly lower number than the Mehlich 3 test — this when the normal is for a Bray 2 test to be more than double the Mehlich 3 result. This appears to suggest that even mineral availability in soil can be modified by the use of the biodynamic preparations.

The only time preparation 501 should be used in hot, dry weather is on hay or silage shortly before cutting, or on ripening fruits and grains, and only if preparation 500 was applied less than three months before. In this situation preparation 501 helps to develop essential oils, sugars and proteins. These are qualities that significantly increase the value of your products. If you don't make a profit you may not be able to continue farming.

In the autumn, apply preparation 500 as a supporting spray, followed by one or two applications of preparation 501 to support the silica process of bringing more light. This will enhance photosynthesis into the darker time of the year. Preparation 501 should be used before grazing if there is any risk of nitrate poisoning or bloat. You can tell whether your system is in balance by whether there are plenty of sugars being produced in the plant, as measured by a refractometer. These sugars flow down the plant and feed bacteria and fungi in the soil around the plant roots. That primary biology then provides food for more carbon-rich organisms like beetles and nematodes, shedding protein as a waste product. This protein is then converted to nitrates in the soil, which transmit oxygen into plants, keeping them growing.

At a recent farm field day in the middle of a wet winter we noted how much dryer the soil and pasture was after it had had an application of a combination spray that contained preparation 501 in its homeopathic form. In a gully paddock where we went to look at some of the herd, the animals came dancing toward us. That morning they had all been seen sleeping on an area where a spray containing preparation 501 had drifted over, in spite of the fact that it was cooler and windier there. The farmer had also noted that his loaded

The result of a living, energetically balanced pasture is lush growth and contented cattle.

tractor was able to get over steeper, wetter ground now — without leaving a mess that would have been the case before he started with the biodynamic preparations.

WORKING WITH THE PLANT LIGHT PROCESSES

In agriculture there has been much focus on the minerals that are taken up by plant roots and less emphasis on the sunlight energy processes that enable photosynthesis to happen. There is also less prominence on the processing or metabolism of the minerals that are taken up too. In biodynamics there is more of a focus and attention given to these light energy processes. In earlier chapters I talked about how the sunlight absorbed by plant leaves enables plants to make sugars and convert nitrates into protein — all very important processes.

During plant growth, the stream of water and dissolved nutrients taken up the plant through the xylem cells is energized by sunlight that has been absorbed by soil silica particles and reflected upwards by clay. The moon's light is also reflected light and assists with carrying nutrition from the soil and all that lives in it up into the plant. When using the biodynamic method we have the potential to moderate the effects of sunlight which affects the whole energy cycle, the activity of soil biology, and availability of minerals. Each preparation carries with it some of the effects of the time it was buried in the soil, and we are able to use them to modify what is happening on the farm.

The horn manure preparation 500 facilitates the activity (processes) of calcium, oxygen and the infrared end of the light spectrum. The results of the use of this preparation suggests better oxygenation and paramagnetic qualities while equally demonstrating the diamagnetic qualities of calcium. Diamagnetic means to push apart and make space; paramagnetic means to draw together. The horn manure strengthens earth energies, providing resistance in the earth, which attracts the light that is needed to grow good food.

The horn-quartz preparation 501 concentrates more of the ultraviolet end of the light spectrum, having a ripening effect on plant life. It pushes life forces back toward the soil, to allow ripening to occur and activating phosphorus which drives the energy cycles. The preparation also assists the phosphorus and vitamin D processes in plants, which relate to shorter wavelength sunlight.

When both of the preparations are used at appropriate times, the light processes through plants are enhanced to enable crop plants to produce a lot of sugars which are transferred down the plant into the roots. Some are then exuded into the surrounding soil to feed soil organisms. These organisms then provide the plants with large quantities of minerals to produce nutrient-dense food. The horn-quartz preparation appears to stimulate enzymes in plant leaves which convert nitrates to high-quality proteins and oils. In this way, high-quality food and fodder can be produced.

Preparation 501 is particularly important for cattle that eat the grass as 501 makes it taste sweeter compared to the bitterness of grass grown with a lot of nitrogen fertilizer that has a high nitrate content. The good taste is an indication of a higher content of nutrients that are essential for producing high-quality meat and milk.

8

Biodynamics & Building Organs

THE aim of biodynamics is to create as much biodiversity as possible and integrate it all into a cohesive unit. Have you noticed that this is how nature works? Rarely do you see just one species on its own. Generally, in the natural woodlands of Europe and the United States, and the New Zealand native bush, there is a mix of many different species of trees, ferns, mosses etc., with many different insects, beetles, spiders, birds and fish living amongst them. Even if your farm specializes in one area, such as dairy or an avocado orchard, you can still build a lot of biodiversity into the shelter belts, pasture, bush and woodlots.

When a farm has been managed well using a biodynamic system, after some years it develops its own unique character or individuality which is appropriate for the particular people, climate, soil and other features of that farm. This can be contrasted with the aim of soluble fertilizer use in farming, which is to make all farms as similar as possible so that they can all be treated according to a single recipe. When you really understand biodynamics you do not just use recipes, you make decisions based on what you see and hear in your environment, and then treat your farm in a way that optimizes its potential.

I remember visiting a small farm in northern Georgia in the United States run by Hugh Lovel. He kept a few cows and grew a diverse range of crops such as corn, soy beans, dwarf beans, and an assortment of vegetables to suit his CSA clients. The farm seemed very much an expression of his personality. It was also very productive. He showed me sweet corn growing very prolifically on land that had not recently been fertilized. The plants were producing so much sugar that it was dripping from the stool roots just above the soil, and also feeding myriads of soil life around the plant roots.

A farm can be thought of as an individual in the same way as a human is an individual. Rudolf Steiner described four bodily aspects of a human: the ego (the "I am-ness"), astral body (the movement, feeling, the soul), etheric body (the flowing life energy), and physical body (the part we all see and what is left when we die).

Steiner's human aspects can easily be related to a farm and the corresponding aspects of a farm are:

The farmer is the ego or the identity part and puts his or her stamp on the farm, making decisions on how and when things happen. Here is where the importance of intention is expressed. How often is a farm referred to as Tom or Albert's place?

The astral body is represented by the birds, bees, and generally all insect and animal life (above and below the soil). In fact the astral body contains all living things in the farm environment.

The etheric body is represented by all that flows within the farm environment. This includes the rain and soil water, and the sap that runs through all plants helping to give form in all its manifestations. It is in this realm that we find the divisions of earth, air, fire and water in the historic way of looking at the world. In the earth element, the plant roots have a similar relationship to the human nerve system. The water element is represented by sap, blood and water in a landscape. The air element is found in soil, water, plants and the lungs of animals and humans. Lastly, the manifesting of warmth in soil, water, air and blood are aspects of warmth or the fire element.

The physical body of the farm can be seen in the mineral elements present in the soil, including carbon, calcium, silica and all the other elements of the periodic chart.

In order to develop your farm as a unique individuality you need a variety of enterprises that complement each other. In the *Agriculture Course* lectures, Steiner said that each farm needs the manure of a large variety of different animals in order to become balanced and complete. When you have the right proportions of different birds, animals and crops they sustain each other and you do not need to bring in any other inputs to the farm. In the New World in particular, farmers have become more and more specialized, many having only one enterprise, such as dairying, poultry, or grain crops. Such farms have to be supported by off-farm inputs because they are characteristically imbalanced.

In a farm individuality, all the parts that make up the whole should be in balance with each other and each body should be in balance within itself to result in a healthy, happy environment that is prosperous in all senses of the word. The farm should be in balance with the surrounding landscape rather than looking like a blot on a page. The farm should also be in harmony with its wider environment, which includes the sun, moon, planets and the stars beyond.

INFLUENCES OF THE MOON, PLANETS & STARS

As our soil and plants move toward a more biological level, the more sensitive they become to the rhythms beyond the Earth's atmosphere. The sun and the moon are the most obvious to us, being the most visible. We can see the moon's influence in the tides and in the changes between neap and spring tides when the full moon and perigee (the point when the moon is closest to the center of the Earth) come together. This is just one of the many rhythms in the solar system of which the earth is a small part.

Our solar system is just a small part of our galaxy of which rhythms are also observable and usable in plant management. The soil's biology embodies a high proportion of water so it also responds to rhythms and movement in the solar system.

In addition, Steiner said that the mineral processes (such as the calcium and silica processes) are affected by energies coming from the planets. The planets that are farther away from the sun than the Earth — Mars, Jupiter and Saturn — affect the silica process, while Mercury, Venus and the moon (the nearer planets) influence the calcium process. Generally we do not think of the planets as having much effect on us on the Earth, but in fact they have a lot of effect on us. And plants are more directly affected by the planets than animals. Animals are mainly liberated from the direct effects of planets because they have independent organs inside, which regulate their body metabolisms.

Many people associate biodynamics with using a moon planting calendar. This can be beneficial, but I generally say to my clients that it is more important to get a job that needs to be done, done at the wrong time according to the calendar, rather than to not get it done at all because you were waiting for the right time. The rhythms of the sun, moon and planets can also be reinforced by suitable use of the biodynamic preparations.

If we want to manage our pasture and crops so that they are less subject to climate changes and the movements of the planets and to provide dependable production, we can use the biodynamic preparations like organs to remedy imbalances and provide a harmonious energy for crops to thrive.

BIODYNAMIC PREPARATIONS AS ORGANS IN THE FARM INDIVIDUALITY

I consider the biodynamic preparation recipes to be the greatest gift any one man has given to humanity. Farmers and growers apply them to their properties as a kind of general tonic, but I believe that Dr. Rudolf Steiner also intended that farmers understand the recipes and use them more specifically to optimize their production. Steiner had instructed Drs. Lily and Eugen Kolisko to work homeopathically with agriculture and commended them for the start they had made by the time the *Agriculture Course* lectures had been given in June, 1924.

Rudolf Steiner also told us about the processes that relate to the energies which work between the planets and the Earth. These energies that help us to build our organs (liver, heart, etc.) in our human bodies are the same or similar to energies which can be harvested through the biodynamic preparations and enable us to build organs in our agricultural entity.

The basic tools of biodynamics are the preparations which act on your farm, stimulating, regulating and harmonizing all the nutrient recycling, growth and production, to optimize the functioning of the whole farm. When we understand how they work, we can use the preparations to bring balance into the system as a remedial measure, as well as their usual supportive role, and thus get maximum productivity.

I believe that we need to become clearly conscious of the functions of each preparation, to how each complements each of the others and how as a whole group they give an overall balance to a farm and the plants and animals in it. Behind each preparation can be seen the working of a planet towards an organ formation — indeed the development of the organs of the agricultural individuality. Doesn't every individuality require organs? When all the organs are healthy and working in balance, we can bring health to our farm as an agricultural individuality — including to the humans working there. With everything working in balance we will then have no organisms that we will be able to describe as pests or diseases. Now, I did not say that it was easy, but you can't get there if you don't make a start.

You can understand more about how to use biodynamic preparations effectively by careful observation of the plants around your farm. With this observation you can then start to understand the dynamics within the matter, rather than just looking at the matter for answers. For example, dandelions can become weeds where hydrogen as ammonia is applied, such as from anaerobic liquid manures or effluent. The energy of this plant can be used in the preparation 506 as a remedy for such situations. The chamomile plant grows in boggy or compacted places where there is no air in the soil, so the chamomile biodynamic preparation can be used to help aerate the soil.

USING COMBINATIONS OF BIODYNAMIC PREPARATIONS

Using the biodynamic preparations is like creating a symphony from just eight notes. In addition to the symphony, you can also play different chords to help restore balance after various imbalancing influences arrive due to the weather or human intervention.

For example, to keep white cabbage butterflies off Brassica (cruciferous vegetable) plants you could use the preparations that draw moisture up around the plant. These could be BD preparation 500, which enhances the calcium activity, supported by the chamomile preparation, BD 503. You could also use the yarrow preparation to stimulate the sulfur process that is prominent in Brassica plants.

Winter pastures need more warmth and light to strengthen stems and enhance oil, sugar and protein production. Equisetum and preparation 501 are helpful for this purpose bringing a summer sunshine effect through the silica process into the leaves. However, it is *most* important that preparation 500 and, if possible, all the compost preparations, have been applied in the *previous two months* to ensure continuous good growth.

EFFECTIVENESS OF THE PREPARATIONS

The quantities of biodynamic preparations used for a specific area tend to vary according to how much is available. In my experience, small quantities, particularly of the compost preparations, are effective, but larger quantities, particularly of preparation 500, are more effective.

I have frequently tested soil by dowsing to see the effects of the preparations. I have found that the length of time the preparations are effective depends a lot upon how much humus the soil contains. In a good soil with a good humus content the effect of the preparations wears off after about three months, but in a silty soil with low humus content, the effect may wear off after only one week.

In later chapters I will discuss the use of the biodynamic practices for specific purposes such as weed, pest and effluent management. But it is important to remember that the primary aim is to use biodynamics to create balance over the whole farm property. Each preparation, acting as an organ, has its own role within the whole organism.

HOMEOPATHIC PREPARATION SPRAYS & RADIONICS

For those who do not have the time or equipment for extensive stirring of the preparations, it is possible to buy them in homeopathic forms which can be added to water while the sprayer is filling and sprayed directly onto plants or soil. Naturally this is more expensive than doing it yourself so a person needs to assess this on a case-by-case basis. The advantage of using this form is that it is effective when the soil is dry (as long as there is green leaf present).

For those who have land that is difficult to drive through and expensive to fly over, there is the option of radionics. This system needs careful management and each person should get instructions for the equipment use from your supplier.

The big advantage of radionics is that there are no wheel marks, it's quick, no diesel or fuel is required, and it can cover large areas effectively. Many Australians living in very dry areas prefer this technology as it seems to be effective in very dry conditions. Depending on the radionic device used, it can be more capital intensive, but still not as costly as flow forms or stirrers and sprayers. I have been using radionics lately as carrying sprayers was no longer possible for me and it has been an interesting learning experience.

One day after a wet spell when our garden was still moist and growing fast, my wife asked if I had been using horn quartz radionically. She pointed to several plants that were growing straight upright, showing signs of going to seed at a time when a lush, more horizontal growth would be expected. Sometimes the effect of the preparations can be as obvious as this. I recently spoke to someone who took part in a field day with me where preparation 500 — and preparation 501 added the next morning — were stirred for participants to take home. The field day attendee later told me that she noted positive differences in her garden the next day.

9

Biodynamic Compost Preparations — Compost, Worm Farms & Barrel Manure

Rudolf Steiner recommended that farmers use the compost preparations in addition to preparations 500 and 501. His descriptions of how these should be made are in lecture five of his *Agriculture Course*. These preparations add energies that complement those of preparations 500 and 501 and in doing so regulate the various minerals (or more specifically the energies or activities of the minerals) that are important for plant growth. I think of them as adding all the colors of the rainbow.

THE COMPOST PREPARATIONS, 502 THROUGH 507

The biodynamic compost preparations bring energies that regulate astral life in the compost, liquid manure or manure heap. This means that they provide an ordering of the otherwise rampant decomposition energies, acting like organs in the compost heap. They work through the whole compost, stabilizing and regulating nutrients, particularly nitrogen, which is otherwise mainly lost as a gas from the pile. When compost or manure made with the biodynamic preparations is applied to the soil it is more effective as less nitrogen has escaped from it. If you add more preparations to the compost within six weeks prior to spreading it over the land, the preparations continue to have a stimulating effect, activating the soil organisms which make nutrient elements available to plants. I once tried treating the soil directly with the biodynamic compost preparations. Near each of the four corners and in the center of a paddock I dug out a spade of soil with cow manure on it and inserted one teaspoon of a compost preparation to the soil. I returned the soil inverted to the hole. The compost preparation was then in close contact with manure, grass and soil. I sprayed valerian preparation over each site. Half the farm was treated in this way and half left as a control. The following three grazing rounds showed a dramatic difference between treated and control areas, evident in both the milk quantity and the quality of the manure on the yard. This is a good way to get the preparations active in the land when you are unable to use them in another way.

Increasing numbers of farmers and orchardists now use homeopathically diluted preparations instead of the set of compost preparations. When using the homeopathically diluted preparations it is important to pour them directly into the compost, not just spray them on top, otherwise they do not work through the compost. These sprays do not have a radiating effect like the solid, stirred preparations. They only work on the soil, compost or plants onto which they are sprayed.

The main purpose of the compost preparations is to be used as a group to regulate decomposition processes in composts and liquid manure. But they can also be used individually as plant medicines when you understand their actions.

502

The yarrow preparation (502) is made from yarrow (*Achillea millefolium*) florets, inserted into a stag's bladder. The preparation is hung in a tree over the summer months where it is exposed to the sunlight and air, then buried in the soil in autumn, and retrieved in the following spring.[1] It has a kidney function — bringing light into the watery, etheric element. Preparation 502 helps to anchor down the sensitivity or intelligence of nitrogen into the watery element in the compost, soil or plant. It also moderates the potassium, sulfur and nitrogen processes.

In lecture three of the *Agriculture Course,* Steiner described the

---

1 For a detailed explanation of how to make this and the other biodynamic preparations discussed here please refer to the book *Grasp the Nettle* by Peter Proctor.

The author picking chamomile flowers for use in making preparation 503.

function of sulfur in activating other elements in a living way. The compost preparations which are active in good quality compost assist with this stimulating activity. The yarrow preparation, and to a lesser extent the chamomile preparation (503), help to activate sulfur in a living way. This is quite different from adding "dead" sulfur as crystals or adding flowers of sulfur.

503

The chamomile preparation (503) is made from German chamomile flowers (*Matricaria chamomilla*) stuffed into a cow's small intestine and buried for six months during the winter. It moderates calcium, sulfur and oxygen activity. It particularly enhances calcium sulfate activity, helping to break up the clay fraction of the soil and enabling plants to obtain more oxygen. It fills and surrounds the plant with fluid like an envelope of moist air or an expansion of the etheric body. This helps the plant to overcome drought stress, this stress which is often indicated by chewing insects becoming pests. These insects are not really pests, just messengers telling you about the condition of your plants.

The chamomile preparation and the cow's horn manure can be used to balance calcium activity. To grow Brassicas of exceptional quality that the cabbage white caterpillar cannot eat, use a good strong biodynamic compost, good levels of calcium and sulfur supported by biodynamic preparation 500, and a little extra preparation 503. When all these measures are in place I have grown large, tasty, bug-free Brassicas even during a hot, dry summer.

504

The stinging nettle preparation (504) is made from common nettle (*Urtica dioica*) by burying it in the soil for twelve months, (generally in a clay tile to contain it and make it easier to find). While the nettle plant is fresh it is rich in calcium. The worms will come and remove the green leaves soon after it is buried in the soil, leaving the silica framework that in due course is harvested as the preparation. The preparation needs to be kept clear of plant roots, as I have had the case where the silica was taken by nettle and grape plants through their roots. In the case of the grape, its roots came under a deep glasshouse footing and travelled almost 11 yards to get to the preparation.

The stinging nettle preparation enhances the light function in the plant and will help it convert nitrogen to the form of amino acids that make up complex protein.

505

The oak bark preparation (505) activates calcium carbonate activity. Calcium carbonate has a contracting action. It is helpful in controlling fungal growth above ground, regulating excessive nitrates and fungi above ground where they are not wanted, and pushing their activity back into the soil. The oak bark preparation has the opposite effect to the chamomile preparation. Sucking insects are also an indicator of excessive nitrate.

To make this preparation, ground English oak bark (*Quercus robur*)

Digging up the nettle preparation 504.

is inserted in an animal skull and immersed in water for six months. The bark from an English oak is used because of the high percentage of calcium it contains. Calcium has a link with water so the skull is set in water for the winter. The water should have some decaying organic matter in it.

506

The dandelion preparation (506) is made by wrapping dandelion flowers in a cow mesentery and burying them underground during the winter. This preparation also assists the availability of elements to plants. Steiner spoke of how it enables the plant to receive what it needs from the environment. Mycorrhizal fungi also assist the plants in gathering elements. The plant, in turn, feeds the fungi with sugars made through photosynthesis.

Preparation 506 helps to develop oils in the plant. This includes the essential oils that provide the plant aroma, and are very important for grazing livestock, particularly for animal reproduction. Preparation 506 also regulates potassium, silica and hydrogen activities.

507

The valerian preparation (507) is made as a valerian flower (*Valeriana officinalis*) extract in water. It regulates warmth, providing a warmth sheath over compost or manure heaps. This preparation can also bring in a saturnine inner warmth to plants upon which it is sprayed. It moderates the effects of frost or cold on plants, having the effect of stretching the plant out. Valerian also moderates the potassium to phosphorus balance.

USING THE COMPOST PREPARATIONS

The compost preparations 502 to 507 may be used in all compost piles, manure piles, liquid manures, effluent systems and liquid manures. For Demeter certification this is required; for other systems this is optional or you may use the homeopathic form if it is more convenient for you. The compost preparations activate and balance the decomposition process so that nitrogen, oxygen and minerals from decaying material are not lost, but are made available as plant food.

USING WASTE MATERIALS TO MAKE VALUABLE SOIL AMENDMENTS

On dairy farms, cow manure is often seen as a waste product that has to be disposed of, whereas in fact it is a valuable resource. Organic waste resources can be enhanced in various forms such as worm farms, static- pile composting, windrow composting, and barrel manure (cow manure piles).

Worm Farms

We generally think of worm farms as aids to home gardening, but they can be used on a larger scale to make valuable liquid fertilizers. One of the most successful organic dairy farmers in New Zealand built up the fertility of his soil using products from his worm farms. He set up several bins into which he put cow manure and some compost worms.

Example of a farm-scale worm farm.

First he waterproofed the bottoms and sides, and then set them on piles so they sloped slightly forward. He ran a gutter along the front of them to catch the liquid that was later spread on the paddocks as a liquid fertilizer. Along with his other innovative practices, this helped him to build one of the best dairy farms in the country. The worms are now working in his soil so well it has given rise to his only complaint. He now says, "The fence posts are all getting shorter!"

Composting

I firmly support the principle of composting for improving soils and for waste management. I have made compost batches of various sizes since I was eight years old and have had several years experience with large-scale composting.

Few farmers make compost, but those I know who have done so have found it well worthwhile. For those who want to develop biodynamics on their farm, it is a good way to spread the influence of the biodynamic compost preparations. Well-made compost raises the humus content of your soil. Humus holds nutrients, preventing them from volatizing or leaching away. A compost heap can also be seen as a high-rise building for biology that can be spread around your farm as a solid or as part of a liquid manure.

In composting I find it is important to have the greater part of the ingredients as fresh green plant material. Animal manure is helpful and generally improves the effectiveness of the finished material. The most important ingredients in any compost are your worst weeds, plus up to 5-15 percent animal manure. Seaweed, if you can get it, is also very good. Mineral elements in rock powder forms are also very beneficial when added to the compost according to the needs shown on your various soil, plant and animal tests. A little lime is generally added to the compost pile. It is important to see that the heap is neither too acidic nor too alkaline for the organisms that you wish to prosper. The right type of lime also helps to prevent nitrogen leaking. The heat of the pile can be governed by the ingredients being incorporated, their particle size, and the size of the heap.

Every farmer should be practicing farm-scale composting.

Compost preparations to be inserted into compost heap.

I insert a level teaspoon of each compost preparation 502 to 506 into a separate hole in the compost heap. They should be kept as far apart as possible when put in liquid manure, so that each preparation can radiate out into the whole heap or brew. When adding the valerian preparation 507, it is stirred in water for about 15 minutes and sprayed over the heap.

An optimum to aim for is one ton (0.9 tonne) of compost to spread for every 2.5 acres (1 hectare) each year. If you can't make enough for that, include a little compost when stirring and spreading liquid manure.

Form & Function — Structure and Shape of Compost and Manure Heaps

One dairy farmer friend uses long windrows and has made enough compost for several years of applications. He turns it as needed with a compost turner and then spreads it over several paddocks.

Windrow length is governed by the quantity of material available or the length of the farmyard or paddock where they are made. If they

This farm-scale compost turner builds and works windrows well.

are too wide and too high they can become anaerobic in the middle. Very large heaps can become compacted and thus will exclude air if they are not constantly turned over. It is very important at all times to ensure that the organisms cultured in the heap have enough oxygen and moisture. If you are using a compost turner, the width and height will be governed by the machine capacity.

For handmade composts, I prefer windrows built in sections on the same site year after year. This enables the good compost organisms to increase as they can move along the heap as the process develops. I find it takes about three years on the same site to get the optimum compost cultures. I like to put a little finished mature compost back into the new heap so that it knows what it should become.

For me the best size is to build cells of about 6 feet x 6 feet (2 meters x 2 meters) and between 3 to 5 feet (1 to 1.5 meters) high. This is big enough to heat up to the optimum temperature and small enough to not need turning and remain aerobic in the center, even when it is covered with a clay paste.

I have recently found that my compost is much improved after covering it with a thin layer of clay paste. This prevents the compost drying out under the hot sun, and the clay is pervious to rain. This apparently provides the right conditions for large, deep burrowing worms. Where the compost has been applied to our soil, these worms burrow down into the clay subsoil, breaking it up.

Cow Pat Pits & Cow Manure Heaps

Making and using cow pat pits has become popular among biodynamic farmers and gardeners in New Zealand as a convenient way to build soil fertility, develop a suitable environment for active and dynamic biology and spread the influence of the compost preparations. An oblong pit is dug about 4 inches (10 cm) deep in the soil. It is filled with good quality cow manure mixed with ground eggshells and basaltic rockdust. The biodynamic compost preparations are added to this. If turned regularly to aerate it, the cow dung should turn into a compost-like consistency after about four months.

I have also found that amendments produced in this way can have a different effect to that which I originally intended. Well-made herbal compost preparations are high in energy and it is important that their effect is contained within the heap. My personal experience with water divining enables me to trace the activity of biodynamic preparations and I have found that when preparations are placed in heaps they are not detectable outside the heap but when they are placed in the ground they will radiate for a considerable distance, thus dissipating much of their energy. I consider, therefore, that preparations placed in a cow manure heap are much more contained and focused on the materials of the heap. I have also observed that sometimes land on which a cow pat pit manure has been spread can lack growth energy. So I now make a dome-shaped heap placed in a wok-shaped depression in the soil. Care needs to be taken that it is not too close to a tree that might send its roots in to rob the manure of all its goodness.

The History of the Cow Pat Pit

Before cow pat pits there was barrel manure, and before barrel manure farmers made liquid manure in a wooden barrel as a fertility amendment. Maria Thun from Marburg, Germany is credited with the invention of barrel manure, an improvement on using liquid manure in a barrel.

There are two things that led to barrel manure and this change. One is that the barrels leaked when some liquid was taken out and the barrel was not immediately refilled as the tops of the staves dried and shrank causing it to leak. The other reason for this change was that there was a need to combat the effects of atomic radiation — a big concern in the Northern Hemisphere during the 1960s and 1970s, until atmospheric testing of bombs was discontinued. Thun found that eggshells and basaltic rockdust were particularly effective at mitigating the effects of radiation so these were added to fresh cow manure, mixed well, then filled into a barrel set into the soil in the garden. Barrels were set one third of their height into the ground and the excavated soil was coved up round the barrel. The barrel then looked like the base of a tree (see lecture four of the *Agriculture Course* in which Steiner explains that this was the ideal form to lead earth energy up into earthy material).

When the manure was placed into the barrel it certainly did not leak but as more air was able to come between the manure and the staves they rotted more quickly so the staves (and later bricks) were used to form a pit in the ground into which to place the manure. The bricks tended to be set in squares rather than the round shape of the barrel. There are not many living things in nature that grow in squares or cube shapes — apart from the common salt crystal, and that is mineral rather than vegetable.

PITS & HEAPS FOR STORING BD COMPOST PREPARATION ENERGIES

In order to retain the compost preparation energies I recommend that the manure/eggshell/basalt mixture be set in a dome in a wok-shaped base scooped into the soil and covered with a plaster of clay after the preparations have been inserted. The ideal shape should be that of eggs, but so far the best I have achieved is a dome over a wok-shaped base. I add a little lime to get the texture that I need to form the dome

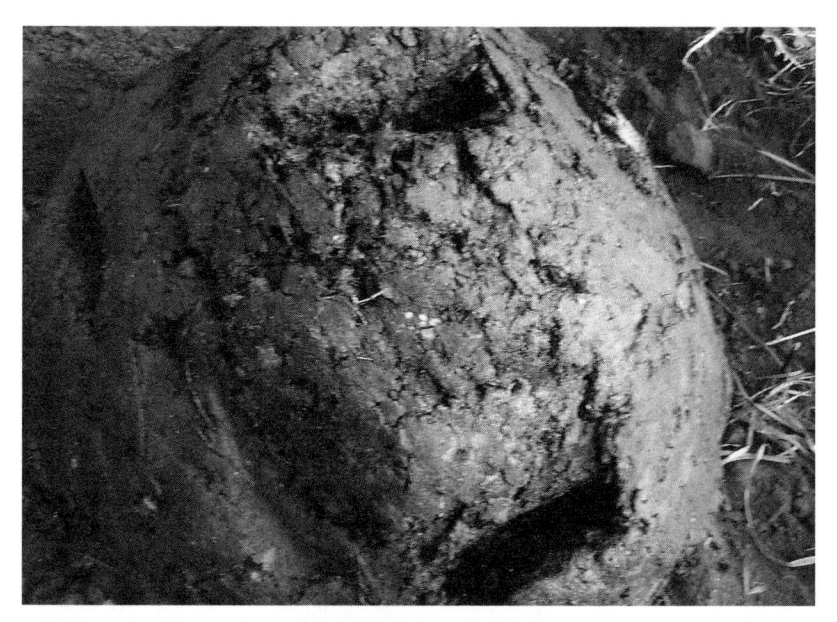

Cow manure heap with holes made for inserting compost preparations.

Cow manure heap finished with clay slurry.

part. I have observed worms using the clay cover to get to the top and work downward into the manure. After using some of the first biodynamic compost preparation I made in this manner, I noted that the clay in our garden was converted to topsoil much more rapidly with a big increase in the number and activity of deep burrowing worms.

I have made small cow manure heaps with several dairy farmers who did not have the equipment to make large compost heaps. When matured, this manure can be used as a concentrate to stir into liquid manure brews. I see the stirring as important to bring rhythm and air into the liquid. These are two very important aspects of life.

LIQUID MANURES

On dairy farms or mixed farms with dairy and pig sheds there will be effluent that some see as a waste product to be disposed of. If managed in the right way, effluent can be formed into a liquid manure with up to four times the value of untreated effluent. This involves adding the biodynamic preparations, quality biodynamic compost, and rhythmical stirring to bring in oxygen and rhythm, both essential ingredients in life.

OTHER BIODYNAMIC PREPARATIONS

Equisetum (Preparation 508) is not one of the compost preparations. An extract of this plant in water is used to strengthen plants against fungal attack. It has a very high proportion of silicic acid and can be seen as a complement to preparation 501 or a partner to the oak bark preparation (505). Preparation 508 is a liquid extract from horsetail *(Equisetum arvense)*.

HORN CLAY

Recently there has been a lot of discussion about horn clay and whether Rudolf Steiner had meant to recommend this as another biodynamic preparation. My father learned biodynamics from Max Karl

(M.K.) Schwartz and Ernst Stegemann, pupils of Steiner in Germany. They taught my father to put a plug of clay in the end of the horn when making preparation 500 or 501. But they did not mention what to do with the clay so I tossed it away when emptying the horns. I now think it was intended to be mixed with those preparations. I have tried this, with good results. Steiner taught that clay helps the transition of energy and nutrients from above to below and vice versa.

Some farmers have made horn clay by filling a horn with clay and burying it either during the summer or during the winter months. According to some, horn clay assists the upward and downward flow of sap through plant xylem and phloem cells, so that what is gathered by the roots is better able to feed the upper plant and vice versa.

The important elements in clay are silica, potassium and aluminum. Iron is also important in yellow and red clays. The aluminum helps to form a reflective layer under the plant which helps stretch the plant out, pushing it into fruiting, which is also part of the silica process. Aluminum restricts the depth to which plants can send their roots. In this respect the clay preparations are closely allied to the valerian preparation.

The clay preparation helps to gather in the winter sunshine, which has a greater proportion of infrared rays than summer sunshine. This type of light assists the digestive process, making silica and potassium more mobile and plants and their fruits larger if in the right proportion to lime and humus. Have you noticed how plants grow differently on clay than on sandy soils?

Clay in the compost helps to form a strong, stable colloid with humus. This is known as the *clay/humus colloid*. When this compost is used it helps plants to grow more strongly, fruit trees produce bigger fruit, and the soil is enabled it to hold more potassium and calcium. This is especially important in sandy or other light soils.

Recently I visited a farm where clay was being used in the spring as a digestive aid. Apparently one day the person applying the clay got the setting wrong and applied twice as much as he was directed to. That patch remained green all through a dry summer. Now at least one fertilizer company I know of adds clay to their fertilizer mixes as a result of this mistake.

10

Weed Management & Plant Peppering

WHAT IS A WEED?

There are several ways to describe a weed. One is that it is a plant that is growing where it is not wanted. The definition is that it is a plant that self-propagates, grows luxuriantly, and is one for which you have not yet found a market. A weed could also be any plant your animals do not wish to eat.

One of the first basic considerations to address when working on any weed or pest issue is your attitude toward the organism that you want to manage. If you regard it as an enemy to be fought and killed you are setting yourself up to fight against nature and in my experience nature often wins. A more effective approach is to love and respect your enemy — and study it. Learn about how it grows, what environment it likes, what niche it fills, and what good it does. You can then think about ways to alter the environment to make it less suitable for that pest or weed and more suitable to what you want to grow. Every organism on earth is a part of the environment and has a role to play and should be respected.

Growing plants protect cultivated, bare soil from the harmful effects of the direct sun. On barren areas that have previously been sprayed with herbicides, pioneer plants such as thistles will grow and help to heal the degraded soil. It is important to understand what is going on and why the plants you consider to be weeds are really there.

WEED MANAGEMENT ON THE DAIRY AND PASTORAL FARM

There are three approaches to weed management open to organic farmers and growers. The approaches are to use an organic herbicide, investigate your soil condition, and try weed deterrents.

The first approach is to find a substitute for the herbicides used by non-organic farmers to kill the weed. There is often a selection of organic products on the market. But these may not be very effective with only one application for persistent weeds like ragwort.

The second approach is to investigate what conditions have led to that weed becoming a problem and work to change those conditions. This will be the most effective long-term solution. Some weeds flourish on compacted, anaerobic soil, while others flourish at a particular soil pH level. You will find that some are able to flourish when a particular trace element is missing. The advice I give to clients about weed management is, "Don't shoot the messenger!" At least don't shoot the weed messenger until you have read the message. Weeds are often an indication that your soil conditions could be improved.

Weeds usually indicate deficiencies of particular minerals in the soil. If the soil is in correct balance, you are less likely to have weed problems. Your objective is to have your desirable plants outcompete those you do not want growing in your field or pasture.

The basic steps in combating weeds through the soil are to:
- Get a good soil and plant tissue (herbage) test.
- Apply minerals to remedy any deficiencies and imbalances of required nutrient elements. This includes not only the major elements like nitrogen, phosphorus, calcium, magnesium, potassium and sulfur, but also the minor elements such as iron, manganese, zinc, copper, cobalt, molybdenum, selenium and iodine.
- Apply seaweed, compost teas, and/or biodynamic preparations to stimulate soil biological activity. See that all elements are present is one aspect, but ensuring that they are *available* to the pasture is equally important.
- Consider using specific biodynamic preparations to change certain conditions.

These basic steps will clear up most weed problems. A farm case study using this approach on a ragwort problem is included at the end of this chapter.

A third approach is to apply a specific deterrent to a particular weed. There are various ways that this can be done.

Make a Weed Tea

Weed teas are made by collecting the problem plant and ramming it into a barrel or an old stainless steel milk vat with a sharp spade. Cover it with water and allow it to stand for ten to fourteen days, depending on the weather and extraction rate. Stir it daily if possible. The important point is to ensure that it does not smell anaerobic. When the water has extracted the essence of the plant then put the water back onto the area from which it came. It may be possible to get two batches of weed tea water from each lot of plant material. When the water extraction is completed the plant material can go into the composting process. Apply about 24 to 26 gallons (90 to 100 litres) of the weed extract per 2.5 acres (1 hectare), diluted in enough water to suit your sprayer.

If possible, spraying should be done in the morning. In general, if you want a spray to be absorbed by any plant leaves, spray in the morning. If you want the spray to go into the soil rather than into plant leaves, spray in the afternoon, and preferably in cloudy weather.

Ragwort is so toxic that it is desirable to take a tea made from it to the anaerobic stage of decomposition so that the toxin decomposes. Doing this the ragwort brew can then be applied with any liquid fertilizer. The first two applications could be as close as a week apart, but a month apart may be more practical. From then on I suggest a three-month interval between applications that would include one just before the main seed germinating periods.

Cutting Back Woody Weeds

Woody weeds generally grow successfully because livestock don't eat them. They grow into large plants which are able to take in plenty of light for photosynthesis and producing lots of sugars, some of which are exuded from the roots to feed the soil biology underneath. The soil biology in turn will help the plant take up more minerals and thrive. To break this cycle you need to prevent the plant from photosynthesizing by removing all the green leaves, so that it cannot feed the biology underneath. The solution is to keep chopping it down. This is most effective at a full moon.

Persistent, weedy gorse growth (a common European weed) can be reduced by applying lime and preparation 500. The plant should then be chopped down several times until it is too weak to grow back. Another effective way of preventing regrowth is to let chickens, goats or sheep graze intensively on the young shoots. These shoots will remain tender for a longer time after the application of lime and preparation 500.

If after you have tried all these approaches you still have a weed problem, then you can try peppering.

WEED PEPPERING

Peppering is the name given to the process of suppressing the germination of a particular type of seed. This effect is usually achieved by burning the ripe plant seed. I will discuss peppering of insects and small animals in Chapter 11.

This method was first described in 1924 by Dr. Steiner in response to a request for help from a group of European farmers. At the time the farmers were greatly troubled by field mice. Further investigation into weed peppering was also carried out by Lily and Eugen Kolisko and published in their book, *Agriculture of Tomorrow*.

This is considered a method of last resort — only to be used when you have first tried to overcome the pest or weed problem by other organic methods such as by changing modifying the environmental conditions to make them less favorable to the pest and have not achieved the desired result.

I have had personal experience with this method of control since 1966. I have successfully used it on buttercups and ragwort weeds; on whitefly, passion vine hopper, Fuller's rose weevil, scale and leaf roller insects; also on rabbits, possums and rats. There are a number of properties throughout New Zealand that are successfully using this method. Whiteflies have been kept out of glasshouses for several years after just one treatment.

When weed peppering, remember that burning needs to be done in exactly the right way, at the right time!

Making a Ragwort Pepper

(Thistles and other plants can be treated in the same way.)

The weed seed must be gathered when ripened fully (or almost fully ripe and left to ripen fully in a paper bag) as if you were saving the seed for reproduction.

The fire is a reversal process that is in effect reversing the germinating capacity of the seed, so the better the seed quality the better the anti-germinating capacity the seed will have. If unripe seed and/or flowers are burned, germination is increased rather than decreased. Collect and dry a little root also, to burn with the seed.

When the seed heads are fully ripe and dry, they must be threshed and cleaned so the seed is not contaminated with too much other plant material. This could be done by beating the seedheads in a thick-walled bag that won't disintegrate when beaten and won't let the seeds escape. With larger amounts seedheads could be beaten between two plastic tarpaulins.

If you are intending to potentize the ash you will need to burn the seed in a container such as a large lightweight frying pan or wok. I would set it over a fairly compact, well-contained fire so that you can stir the ash without getting burned. A little root may be added, but no other plant part. In burning, the aim is to get as much black ash (carbon) as possible and as little white ash (potassium hydroxide) as possible. You could also burn on a small twig fire set on the ground. I would suggest digging out a wok-shaped fire hole in a relatively sheltered place that will be safe from setting anything else alight. Once finished with a twig fire, sieve out the bits of twig from the ash as they do not contribute to the process.

The ash should be mixed by hand with a carrying agent like sand or crusher dust. Larger quantities can be mixed in a concrete or a dry fertilizer mixing facility — whichever best suits your purpose and scale of operation. I suggest that you put 6 to 7 ounces per acre (400

Making ragwort pepper.

to 500 grams per hectare) but I have seen an effect with as little as 4 ounces (110 grams) of possum ash dropped in sand from an airplane. Hand spreading was more effective though and was still protecting the property eleven years later.

The timing of weed peppering can also be an additional help in combating the problem. Seeds generally germinate best at full moon. Since ragwort frequently germinates in the autumn and in the spring, the suggestion is to use the autumn full moon as a time to burn the well prepared seed.

If you have a small amount of seed relative to the area to spread it on you may need to potentize the ash, using standard decimal homeopathy, as follows:

The potentizing process is begun by stirring 0.03 ounces (one gram) of the ash with 0.3 ounces (nine grams) of milk sugar for one hour.

This process is known as trituration. This material is considered to be 1X potency. There would be 10 grams of the 1X then mixed with water to make 100 ml of 2X potency. After mixing the liquids are shaken rhythmically for about three minutes. Then take the resulting 100 ml and add 900 ml of water, shaking rhythmically again, to make 1 litre total which is now 3X potency, and so on, until you reach the desired dilution rate. 8X dilution has been found to be effective and is often recommended, so the dilution process is often continued to 10 litres of 4X, 100 litres of 5X, 1,000 litres of 6X, 10,000 litres of 7X and a final amount of 100,000 litres of 8X dilution. This is spread at 3.4 to 6.8 ounces per acre (250 to 500 ml per hectare).

The effect of potentized ash wears off quickly, so ideally you should spread it several times a year. The nature of homeopathy is to use small doses frequently to achieve an effect over time when working toward a new homeostasis, or steady state. While an effect may be observed soon after the first application, it may take up to four years to fully get the result that you wish to achieve. The potentized material may be applied with any liquid fertilizer. The first two applications could be as close together as a week apart, but a month apart may be more practical. After the first two applications I suggest a three-month interval that would include applications just before the main germinating periods.

A WEED CASE STUDY

Ragwort (Jacobaea vulgaris, syn. Senecio jacobaea)
Why does ragwort grow so prolifically on certain soils?

A few years ago I was asked to assist with the management of a heavy ragwort infestation on dairy farm paddocks in the Bay of Plenty on the northern coast of New Zealand's North Island. Upon investigating why ragwort grew so prolifically, the first thing that I noticed was that the soil around the roots of the weed plants was very different than the soil around the neighboring grass roots. The soil around the ragwort roots was more alive with worms and other organisms than the soil around the grass roots. This was investigated widely on the farm and was con-

A trial of biodynamic control of ragwort underway.

firmed by other farmers and their staff. We then measured the brix reading of the leaf sap in the ragwort plants and the grass growing close by. In every case the brix measured in the grass was half that of the ragwort plant in the same pasture. The farmer bought a refractometer for his assistant to make further observations. The results were always the same.

The next tests were taken from a typical ragwort plant and pasture 31 inches (800 mm) apart, aiming for similar fertility areas in relation to cow pats, urine etc. Plant tissue (herbage) samples of each were taken, then a soil sample was taken from the root zones of the same plants. In analyzing the results I looked for where the results were noticeably different. I also noticed readings that showed little difference between the samples.

A very noticeable difference in the soil test (Table 1) was that the nitrate N availability was much higher under the ragwort plants than under the grass in the rest of the pasture. This was consistent with the higher brix readings for the ragwort plants and the visual observation that there was much more biological activity happening under the ragwort plants. Clearly the ragwort plants were exuding more sugars to feed biology around the roots which in turn released more nitrate nitrogen. More fungus was also discernible around the ragwort roots than from around the grass roots.

TABLE 1. *Pasture & Ragwort Soil Test Results*

SOIL TEST	UNITS	RAGWORT SOIL	PASTURE SOIL
pH		6.4	6.0
Calcium	kg/ha	3008	2609
Magnesium	kg/ha	236	171
Potassium	kg/ha	197	75
Sodium	kg/ha	136	69
Aluminum	kg/ha	8	11
Phosphorus (Bray 2 test*)	ppm	186	150
Boron	ppm	0.6	0.39
Copper	ppm	1.07	0.82
Zinc	ppm	4.29	5.56
Molybdenum	ppm	0.63	0.51
Nitrate N	ppm	14.5	5.4

* *The Bray 2 test indicates soil reserves of phosphorus, in comparison to the Mehlich 3 test which is a softer extraction, giving a better idea of the level of phosphorus available to the plant. In New Zealand the Resin P. test has a similar score to Mehlich 3. Often in a soil test where Merlich 3 shows 55 ppm the Bray 2 test will show 120 ppm.*

Looking at the plant tissue sample results (Table 2), there are noticeable differences in one of the major elements — the potassium (potash) results. Then, in the minors elements, boron is the most noticeably different, with over twice as much in the ragwort sample (31.9 versus 14.8 for the grass). The next most noticeable difference is with the aluminum, with much more in the ragwort (615.1 versus 451 ppm in the pasture grass sample). There is also slightly more iron, manganese, copper and zinc in the ragwort plant sample. When there are large discrepancies between mineral levels measured in soil and pasture tests it is a good indication that there is not much soil biology activity, particularly fungal activity.

The high aluminum content in the ragwort would contribute to its toxicity and unpalatability to cattle, so they leave it to grow for longer

TABLE 2. *Pasture & Ragwort Plant Tissue (Herbage) Results*

PLANT TEST	UNITS	RAGWORT LEAF	PASTURE LEAF
Nitrogen	%	3.34	3.41
Phosphorus	%	0.41	0.39
Potassium	%	3.13	2.15
Calcium	%	1.02	1.05
Magnesium	%	0.20	0.29
Sulfur	%	0.25	0.30
Boron	ppm	31.9	14.8
Iron	ppm	344.1	277.4
Manganese	ppm	84.3	97.5
Copper	ppm	8.7	8.1
Zinc	ppm	44.9	37.2
Aluminum	ppm	615.1	450.9
Molybdenum	ppm	3.8	4.1
Cobalt	ppm	1.4	1.3

periods, enabling it to photosynthesize more than the grass that is regularly grazed down.

Looking at all these figures leaves me with the suggestion that the percent of potassium needs to be reduced and the copper and zinc levels need to be increased to change the dynamics of the pasture so that the pasture grows more prolifically.

The farmer is now working to apply lime, copper and fish fertilizer as well as compost teas. Homeopathic biodynamic preparations have also been added on several occasions. He has also liquid composted the ragwort plants on several occasions trying to reduce the incidence of ragwort as well as burning the seeds and spreading the ash back over the land. The ragwort continues to grow well.

Given that there may be different relationships between the soil and weeds among different soils, the above method can be used to test what the plant relationship is in your soil.

11

Using Biodynamics to Manage Pests & Disease, Animal Peppering

Pests and diseases are the focus of considerable attention in horticulture and agriculture. The teachings by Rudolf Steiner give us a different approach from the combative approach used by most growers. Steiner gave us a means of understanding the conditions that favor particular pests and diseases and how we can alter those conditions to manage the problem.

When we observe plants and animals carefully we can look for what is different between a healthy and a so-called diseased plant or animal, or one that is being attacked by insects, bacteria, virus or fungi. In this chapter I will focus mainly on plant pests and diseases. Similar principles to these can be applied to animal health. I will discuss some aspects of animal health in Chapter 12.

UNDERSTANDING PLANT GROWTH

The first thing we see when viewing a plant is its physical manifestation, but that is not what constitutes the whole plant. Steiner, in the biodynamic agriculture lectures that he gave to farmers in June of 1924, spoke about other unseen aspects of the plant. One, he termed the "etheric" body. This corresponds to the etheric body of a human, referred to in Chapter 8. This is the unseen living, flowing energy that produces the plant that you can see. The etheric body is a body of very delicate and fine water vapor that fills and surrounds the physical body. Some people see "auras" around plants which emanate from the etheric body. While I don't personally see the etheric or water body of plants I can see the effects of these. The plant does its best to fill most of the space of its etheric body with its physical body.

The etheric body forms an envelope for the plant to grow into and helps to draw water into the plant mostly from below. The etheric body also draws in carbon dioxide and oxygen from the atmosphere. Pests often appear when the etheric body is not growing at the same rate as the physical plant body. By balancing the etheric body with its physical body, a certain degree of pest management can be achieved.

When growth conditions are very good, the etheric body grows faster than the physical body can fill it, which then provides a space for fungus or sucking insects to live.

If the weather suddenly turns hot and dry the etheric body shrinks and the physical plant will have periods of wilting and may eventually begin to look a bit wizened. As the etheric body withdraws the astral body can move in. This brings about the impulse to flower. If this process goes too far chewing insects get the message, "Here is a good meal" and they drop in for a feed.

The "astral" or air body exists like a cloud around and above the plant. This body provides the energy for fruiting and seeding in plants and for movement and feelings in animals. Where astral body energy touches a plant gently, flowering occurs. This is often after there has been strong plant growth that has drawn back a little. The astral body is then able to dip in and touch the plant. When the astral body presses in more strongly, as when there is drought stress, chewing insects come in. Often this is in the form of an insect that lays eggs that turn into hungry grubs that will feed on the plant. In other cases the plant will produce alkaloids that are poisonous to animals and humans. Bacterial infections can also occur, or if the temperatures are warm enough, blights will also occur.

The "ego" or warmth body is even more tenuously connected to the plant. It fosters the seeding process and in some plants a small element of cyanide develops. Where this activity is excessive, as in tomatoes in the autumn, I have seen looper caterpillars turn up.

When farmers have a simplistic concept of feeding plants — left over from the early days of Justus von Liebig where we feed plants with large helpings of water-soluble salts, particularly those based around nitrogen — the plant becomes stressed as none of its energy bodies can function well. When this happens the plant calls in the garbage collectors. Many of the organisms that we term pests are simply telling us that a particular plant is not fit for us and is lacking in high-quality nutrition in its present state. We then behave as if the problem is a lack of poisons and smother the plant with substances that are toxic to this or that organism (and often ourselves as well). Aren't we supposed to be the most intelligent beings on the planet? Isn't it about time that we worked out what the cause of the problem really is and correct it at the most basic level?

Often plants are weak and easily attacked by pests if they cannot obtain the minerals they need in the right balance from the soil. Amending the soil can help. Or there may be an imbalance between the energies of the different plant bodies described above. This can occur when there are weather extremes such as having too much rain or being too hot and dry. These situations are when applying biodynamic preparations can help the plant cope with the extremes.

The problem could also be a lack of oxygen in the soil that can occur when applied fertilizers oxidize, such as when ammonia is oxidized to nitrate and oxygen is then taken from the soil faster than it can be added through plant respiration. This impacts the aerobic organisms that make nutrients available to plants. It can also lead to nutrient deficiencies that in turn can lead to diseases and pest attacks.

USING BIODYNAMIC PREPARATIONS IN PEST MANAGEMENT

The preparations 500 and 501 can often be used to reduce the effects of extreme weather on plants. I often use these preparations strategically in particular conditions and find them very useful. When they are used to bring conditions into balance, there is less likelihood of pest and disease issues. I have already described in previous chapters how the preparation 500 assists with the flow of watery, calcium-charged growth energies up into plants from the soil. This has the effect of strengthening the etheric or water body of the plant. The preparation 501 has the opposite effect drawing a plant up into the light, into the astral area around it.

There are several considerations to bringing more light into a plant — the various growth aspects need to be balanced. Always consider the plant as a living, dynamic organism. Applying preparation 501 may help but it might make the situation worse if the plant is lacking calcium. Calcium energy, which is strengthened by applying preparation 500, forms a receptacle into which light is poured into the plant. This is why it is so important to apply preparation 500 first, before any preparation 501 is applied.

When sucking insects are attracted to plants that have grown too quickly and/or contain a lot of nitrates, more light is needed in the plant. Light activates enzymes that convert nitrates to amino acids and complex, or true, proteins. Insects are unable to digest protein, so well-grown plants high in protein are left alone. Growing such plants has the double benefit of producing good food for us and our animals and solving your pest issue.

Preparation 501 and/or a tea made from equisetum or horsetail (preparation 508) are often effective when sprayed to manage fungal diseases. This is because they have the effect of pushing down the etheric envelope around the plant. The oak bark preparation 505 can also have a similar effect by drawing the nitrates and etheric envelope back into the ground.

Several manufacturers now sell homeopathically diluted biodynamic preparations specifically for the purpose of balancing the plant's physical, etheric and astral bodies. Some of these products are even suitable for spraying on plants for specific pest problems such as chewing insects or for fungal diseases.

USING SOIL MINERAL BALANCING & SOIL BIOLOGY IN PEST MANAGEMENT

The soil mineral balancing concept introduced by Dr. William Albrecht is a way to maintain plants and animals in good health so they can resist pests and disease. From observations of where buffalo preferred to graze, Albrecht developed indicators of how mineral elements should relate to each other in the soil and plants in order to maintain good healthy pasture. The preferred grazing areas also were found to have better populations of soil organisms. Those organisms we can see are indicators of the state of health of any soil. We all accept that a good worm population is indicating a healthy soil. If we have pathogens like root-feeding nematodes, army worms or grass grubs, we know something is out of balance and we should assess if there is something we can do to improve the situation. In these situations there is often a mineral imbalance in relation to the ideal for the plants we wish to grow. If we correct the mineral imbalance, the plant disease or pests will leave.

FERTILITY REVERSAL OR PEPPERING

In Chapter 10 I described the peppering method for managing weeds. The same method can be used for animal and insect pests. Rudolf Steiner gave us indications to use peppering as a last resort, only if all other methods did not work. Peppering has been used by biodynamic farmers for many years to keep animals such as mice, rabbits or possums away from pastures, orchards and gardens.

A very important principle to keep in mind when working with peppering is to respect the organism you want to manage. Even the worst agricultural pest is part of Creation and has a role to play. The pest has gotten out of balance, which is often caused by man. It may have been moved somewhere where there are no natural predators, or the perfect environment for it has been inadvertently created. For example, rats have the role of clearing up rubbish and if you leave food lying around they come to deal with it. Pests may also be attracted to people who have particular thoughts, disease conditions or emotions. For example, rats seem to be drawn to be near people with digestive issues, and I have seen mice attached to people who are nervous.

We should aim to live in peace and harmony with all other organisms on the earth.

Peppering is a way of communicating your intention to the group soul of a species. If you communicate your respect of the organism and recognize its right to exist in a suitable environment and then respectfully ask it to move away from the area that you are treating, you are more likely to be effective than if you do it with a feeling of hatred toward the species.

I have had personal experience with this peppering method of control since 1966. As I said previously, I have successfully used it on buttercups and ragwort in plants, and whitefly, passion vine hopper, Fuller's rose weevil, scale and leaf roller in insects. I have also had success using it with rabbits in several areas of New Zealand. On each occasion that rabbits were treated, it took six weeks for them to move, they then stayed away for about twelve months before they returned. After the second peppering treatment they stayed away for two or more years. If they come back again a third treatment works for a much longer period.

I have also had success with peppering possums in New Zealand. In one instance we burned 90 skins, mixed the ash with sand and spread it over 494 acres (200 hectares) of bush from a fixed wing airplane. People living in the area noticed a lot of possum movement shortly after this, and there was less damage from possums for several years afterword until heavy rains seemed to have washed away the effects. In the same year (2000), 3.5 ounces (100 grams) of this possum skin ash was mixed into almost 8 tons of sand and spread by hand sparingly round the boundary of a 70-acre property that had been cleared of possums by poisoning. This property still remained clear of possums for ten years until retreatment. The possum populations in the neighboring areas appeared to increase for a year or so but after several years they decreased as the margin increased around the treated area.

The Method for Small Animals

Peppering involves burning possum or rabbit, rat or other animal skins at a favorable astronomical time. The method requires an understanding of how energies from the planets and the zodiac affect life on earth. We are well aware of the impact of the sun and moon on planet Earth, but we have a lesser understanding of the impact of the planets

The author's mother Nancy helping prepare possum skin ash.

and the constellations on Earth. The appropriate alignment of Venus at the time of burning is necessary if the method is to work well. This timing has been much discussed and the general consensus is that Venus should have the constellation of the Scorpion behind it from our point of view from Earth. The preferred time is after the superior conjunction with the Sun. This does not mean that the process does not work at any other time. I have found that pepper from burning at less suitable times can still be effective. Another aspect to consider in this type of work is your intention. This is an opportunity to talk respectfully to the ego or identity that stands behind the organism that you consider to be a pest.

When peppering animals it is important to use skins of animals which have reached reproductive age. I also prefer to use females. The relationship between Venus and the feminine aspect is well known — all female animals relate to Venus. When Venus is in front of the constellation of Scorpio, reproduction of animals is affected. A skin collected and carbonized by fire can hold the message relating to that animal's fertility. Reproduction is core business for most animals so they will leave unfavorable areas if it is at all possible. The ash only affects animals of the species of which the skin is burned.

Burn the skin to leave only carbon which can hold a message. Put your well-intentioned message into the carbon.

The carbon obtained from the burnt skin of the possum interferes with the reproductive energy of the possum only. In animals the skin is the sense organ of the reproductive system. Fire is the antithesis of fertility and water supports it. I have noticed that if there is rain shortly after spreading the ash the treatment seems to be ineffective. This has been noticed with possums and when having different people spreading parts of the same ash mix at different times and places. The consistent difference between where the treatment acted as a deterrent and where it was ineffective was how long the weather was clear after spreading the ash. This is an initial observation. I therefore suggest that you check the long-term weather forecast before spreading, and for further security spread no more than half of your pepper on the first application.

The ash is mixed with sand or other suitable carrier and spread very thinly on damp ground. I have found that the soil needs to be moist and that the atmosphere needs to have a condensing process rather than evaporative process at the time — rather like the conditions you would choose to apply horn manure, preparation 500. For all organisms the soil is the holder of the peppering influence.

Some property owners have applied the ash to the whole area to be treated, while others have applied it to the boundary of an area they wished to protect. When they shared experiences of how many years protection was provided, the results of how often the treatment was repeated have varied. The animals treated did avoid the area, as if staying in the area could reduce their fertility. It is much easier to stop an animal from re-entering an area than to chase it out or stop it from breeding within the area. Animals have habits and are naturally reluctant to leave their territories.

When I have only a small quantity of ash I sometimes dilute it homeopathically in sand or distilled water, as described earlier in this book. When using the potentized ash, treatment may have to be a little more frequent. When you work with a homeopathic substance you should keep using it until you observe a change, then stop and re-assess. If you potentize a pepper, the effect doesn't last as long — generally for about 12 months, so repeated applications may be required.

Peppering Insects

When working with peppering animals you should consider the zodiacal background behind the sun as this has an effect on animals. When treating insects the constellation behind the sun's position is the most important timing consideration. The most favorable time for peppering insects is during the months when the sun is moving between the constellations of Capricorn through to Cancer. The Capricorn end suits soft insects. The harder the insect and its shell, the closer to Cancer the sun needs to be. This applies in both the Northern and the Southern Hemispheres. I have noticed that in Germany and New Zealand flies are most prolific in the same month, showing that it is the background of the Sun rather than the season that affects them.

It helps if you understand the organism you are dealing with and its life cycle. When do they breed most actively? When are they easiest to catch? Light traps are very effective for night-flying insects. For day-flying insects, battery-powered vacuum cleaners have been used. For other insects, like those I found in a kiwi fruit orchard, I used a large plastic sheet on the ground then tapped the support wires. When the insects felt the vibrations they dropped to the ground. I swept them together then scooped them into a jar and screwed on the lid. Ground crickets can be caught in a bucket place in the ground with some molasses and meal as bait. I cut a hole in the lid so they can climb in, but can't get out.

Catch and burn the entire insect as they are rather difficult to skin and their eggs don't amount to much. For treating commercial orchards I have homeopathically diluted the ash using Maria Thun's recommendation of the eighth decimal (8X) potency. Others have tried different potencies with success.

It is important to note what conditions so ideally suit an insect that it becomes a pest. We should do all that we can to change the conditions to suit the organisms we wish to flourish and which are the least accommodating to those we consider pests. It is no good peppering crickets unless you change the soil conditions, otherwise they will quickly re-infest the soil. This is a point to consider for all organisms that you pepper. Insects, animals and plants should be managed as much as possible by changing the habitat or the environment. The wise use of the biodynamic preparations may well be helpful to achieve this outcome.

12

Animal Health Management

To keep your animals in good health, think about their native environment. Cows like lush pastures with trees to stand under and browse. Pigs like bushy land to root in — they need to eat soil. Alpacas' native pastures are in high elevations with marshy, stony land containing scrubby bushes and a few trees, and lots of bright light. Look for ways to provide habitat with similar conditions to their native environment.

There is no single recipe for soil and pasture management to keep your animals healthy — every property is unique. Following the principles for soil and pasture management discussed in earlier chapters should result in healthier animals. Many of the organic dairy farmers I know have very minimal veterinary bills because they observe the basics of balancing minerals in the soil. Often this starts with lime to increase the calcium level. All biology in the soil needs calcium for their bodies and to provide the lubricants to move easily through the soil. Calcium though needs to be balanced with magnesium, potassium and sodium and activated by sulfur and boron. Whenever calcium/lime is applied, you should ensure that zinc, copper and cobalt are also keeping pace for a better chance of healthy animals.

Trees are an important part of any farm for shelter, shade, fodder and medicine. Trees and shrubs are part of the traditional diet of almost all of our domestic animals. Most farms don't have anywhere near enough trees and shrubs. Up to 30 percent of a farm can be covered by a variety of trees so animals can obtain the best range of nutrients in their fodder.

Good balance of trees in pasture. Up to 30 percent of a farm can be covered in trees, all to the benefit of the livestock.

Cascading trees like weeping willows grow down toward the animals, whereas trees with a more upright habit may need pruning to make the fodder available. Some farmers put branches through a chipper and find that most of what is fed to their animals is eaten. In some cases the trees can be repeatedly coppiced — cut to ground level and allowed to branch from the stump — and the branches taken to fed the livestock. Well-managed systems can result in extra total growth from trees and pasture production and also extra profit.

Another benefit of trees is to slow the wind so that the carbon dioxide exhaled by grazing animals is not blown away before the plants can breathe it in again. The largest part of most plants is made up of oxygen and carbon. Carbon dioxide might therefore be considered an important plant nutrient, not just a greenhouse gas that some are taxed for producing.

Herbs are plants that we do not consume in bulk. We need to be able to have access to them periodically, when they are needed. Most animals know this instinctively. In many modern pastures, though they are classified as weeds and sprayed with herbicide.

The pasture should contain a large variety of grass species. In bio-

Deep, diverse pasture is the best food and medicine for cattle.

logical agriculture we talk of diversity in many ways, and this also includes pasture species. If plants grow well and your animals eat it and perform well on it, they why not grow it? Our domestic farm animals, like us, need the eight essential amino acids. To have all these supplied sufficiently, a good variety of tasty well-grown plants are required. A complex protein is made up of a variety of amino acids that varies between plants. Too often we see protein described as N multiplied by 6.25. This form includes simpler nitrogenous compounds such as nitrates that, when eaten by animals and humans, are toxic in that they inhibit the blood's capacity to carry oxygen to the muscles and organs. I have heard it explained that the alteration of the biology this causes in the gut leads to an increase in the quantity of methane given off. In a lower oxygen environment pathogens thrive much better than the organisms associated with good health. We should do everything we can to maintain a well oxygenated environment inside and outside of ourselves and our animals.

A further aim in pasture management should be to optimize photosynthesis through careful management of the grazing rotation. I have often seen large herds of cows grazing on grass that is too short. When the rotation frequency is long enough for the pasture to grow higher,

Cattle can relax in shade on a hot day.

there is more leaf available to take in more light to create more grass and better quality nutrients. More sugars are also sent to the roots as the grass leaves grow longer, enabling a much quicker regrowth after grazing too. By using biodynamic preparations the farmer can keep high-quality, palatable green leaf on the pasture longer.

MINIMIZING STRESS

When you keep animals as close as possible to their natural environment, with minimum stress, they are much better able to keep healthy. There may still be disease conditions or parasites that prey on them, and often this is when the mineral energies and/or their body energies are not balanced. When this happens you might have to treat the disease immediately, but you also need to consider what conditions may have caused it and how you can change those conditions. Successful biodynamics involves careful observation and learning about the physical and energy conditions that favor particular disease organisms.

Rubbing posts are very important for cattle (and most animals). How often do we also like a good rub or a scratch?

Some Examples of Managing Specific Conditions

Barber Pole Worm (*Haemonchus contortus*) is so called because the female's ovary is wrapped spiral fashion around her 1- to 2-mm body like a barber's pole. Of all the intestinal worms attacking sheep and goats, this is the most prolific egg layer and breeder. The eggs are deposited on the ground with sheep's feces. They move quickly onto grass to be ingested during warm, moist weather. They attach themselves to the lining of the abomasum, or fourth stomach of a ruminate, and suck blood. Large numbers of them can cause the death of the animal; lesser numbers cause various degrees of ill thrift and breaks in the wool.

The suggested action is to ensure a good balance of all minerals commonly considered important to soil, plant and animal health. This will ensure a stronger and more resilient animal. Feeding extra protein (like fish meal) can help the sheep thrive while poor-quality pasture leaves the sheep at greatest risk. High-quality protein with a good balance of all the essential amino acids along with good carbohydrates

A healthy, contented cow.

with all the essential sugars represented will make the animal's blood less palatable to intestinal parasites, and quite likely many of the external parasites as well.

The most important minerals to have in your pasture to help provide resistance to barber pole worms are a sufficient quantity and quality of phosphorus, copper and cobalt. Phosphorus hardens tissue, making it harder for the worms to suck blood out. Seaweed drenches have also been observed to help. Some of the effective ingredients in seaweed are selenium that helps to repair broken tissue by encouraging good blood flow into muscle tissue and zinc which is the most plentiful element in seaweed extract and helps with the immune system. Kelp, from which most seaweed extracts are made, contains an essential sugar that is not readily found elsewhere.

Bloat is a common problem when the forage-to-concentrate dry matter ratio is too low. Generally, when feeding predominantly corn silage

Shrubs and trees provide food, shelter and medicine to your herd.

diets, do not reduce dry matter to below 55 percent of the ration. When feeding haylage diets, dry matter should be at least 40 to 45 percent of ration.

Animals receiving rations that cause chronic bloat do poorly as ruminal pH is too low (too acidic), and normal digestion of nutrients is impaired and further feed intake is minimal.

When cows consume large amounts of certain legumes such as fresh, lush alfalfa and clover, they may suffer a frothy, acute form of bloat.

I also have seen bloat that appeared to be related to excessive molybdenum in the soil. The molybdenum causes excessive growth of the nitrogenase bacteria that live in nodules on clover roots and fix nitrates from atmospheric nitrogen for the clover. Excessive supply of nitrates in pasture leads to too much acid in the stomach of the animals that eat the clover. In my opinion nitrates are a major influence on bloat gases in the stomach. Nitrates easily convert to nitrites in the body, and nitrites block synthesis of vitamin A. For many reasons pastures containing plenty of amino acid variety in proteins are very important in the diet at all levels.

Bicarbonate of soda may be a short-term solution to bloat and can be used as a drench. The corrective measure at the soil level for excessive molybdenum is to apply sulfur or copper sulfate as a spray on pasture after grazing. Copper sulfate seems to be the most effective. To lessen its harshness on soil biology it could be dissolved or chelated into liquid seaweed, or perhaps a slurry made of cow manure, then applied as a spray after grazing. This should correct the problem for the following grazing.

On the farm where excessive molybdenum was a problem, preparation 501 or horn quartz was also applied to the pasture to assist the pasture plants to convert crude N or nitrate to a complex of amino acids. Don't forget that preparation 501 can only be applied to pasture where preparation 500 has been applied in the previous six weeks.

ALPACA HEALTH

Alpaca farming has become quite popular in recent years, both in New Zealand and internationally. I have been asked to visit several alpaca farms in New Zealand where the alpacas were not thriving. Generally I have found that the conditions were not suitable for the animals. They were expected to eat a lush ryegrass pasture, in contrast to the poor grasses and bushes of their native habitat. Alpacas are also extremely affected by the nitrates in pasture. To understand this we must first look at where alpacas are native and the conditions under which they have developed.

The Altiplano of South America, where alpacas originated has poor soil, a lower percentage of oxygen in the air, and a higher proportion of ultraviolet radiation in the light spectrum. There appears to be a connection between ultraviolet light and phosphorus, and this lies behind my recommendation to use horn quartz or preparation 501. Pampas grass is also a good source of phosphorus.

The other element that relates to light and photosynthesis is magnesium. Magnesium is the mineral used in emergency signal flares. Adequate magnesium is very important for alpacas. When it is inadequate they will nod their heads and appear a little drunk. Many alpaca farmers have an issue with staggers, which is related to magnesium deficiency, when ryegrass phytotoxin is not the main cause. Magnesium deficiency also reduces the ability of plants to photosynthesize, so plants take in less light and are less able to process nitrates into protein. Resowing the pasture with a mix of grass species and beneficial herbs, such as plantain and chicory, is likely to improve alpacas' health.

For alpacas there appear to be two main elements of concern: phosphorus and magnesium. But these elements are among many that are important in soil, plants and animals. Not only do we need to ensure there is enough of each element, the ratio of one to another is crucial.

DRY COW MANAGEMENT

When drying cows off, feed them on minimal grass and enough hay to equal 95 percent of their maintenance ration for one week to ensure milk supply is totally stopped. Then keep the cows on a gently rising plane of nutrition using mostly dry feed, i.e. hay or baleage. During the cold, wet part of the year, the warmth of hay made in the summer heat is a natural balance. Musty hay should be avoided at all costs. Many farmers no longer make hay and feed silage instead. Silage does not provide the warmth that hay does, so is less suitable for cold, wet days. It is important to keep cows' udders clean until plugs have been formed in the milk ducts in the teats.

Milk fever (hypocalcemia): This condition reflects a lack of vitamin D, inadequate absorption of calcium, and an excess of protein. The preventative remedy for this condition is to feed a higher proportion of good quality hay in the period preceding calving. Animals make vitamin D when exposed to sunshine.

Good-quality hay is made during maximum summer warmth and sunshine. It is nourishing but low in proteins. If you are not intending to make hay, perhaps consideration should be given to purchasing sufficient quantities for supplementing cow nutrition leading up to calving, to reduce the risk of milk fever in future years. If cows are held in covered barns they should be let out whenever there is sunshine in the middle of the day to increase the absorption of vitamin D.

The application of preparation 501 (horn quartz) to the pasture should increase the vitamin D effect. This may be applied on the days leading up to grazing, but only when you have already applied the other biodynamic preparations. In winter the effect is stronger the closer to midday that it is applied. The time in the morning that it is applied changes how gently or harshly it works.

Soft feet is often a challenge. It relates to a low uptake of zinc. Drinking water may be high in iron and manganese, making it more difficult for cows to absorb elements like zinc, cobalt, copper, sodium, potassium, magnesium and calcium. Zinc is best given in chelated form. As with all minerals, once the immediate health problem has been resolved after feeding it direct to the animals, it is better to apply the minerals to the soil. This can be done directly or via compost or liquid manures, so the animals ingest the minerals through the pasture.

13

Dairy Farm Effluent Management

ARE your effluent ponds smelly? Are the paddocks that are sprayed with effluent becoming weedier?

Effluent needs to be seen as a valuable resource and handled accordingly. An efficient farm should not allow nutrients to either leach as nitrate or evaporate as ammonia or methane gas. If this does happen, then your farm has got the agricultural version of leaky gut syndrome. How efficient is it to buy nutrient inputs and allow them to leak away or volatilize?

USING BIODYNAMIC PREPARATIONS

The use of biodynamic preparations can help to manage and recycle barn or other kinds of effluent with the benefits of reduced smell and increased pasture growth — making it a valuable fertilizer on your land. The biodynamic compost preparations are added to activate microorganisms and act to aerate the slurry. The objective is to stabilize the nitrogen content for a slower, controlled release over time.

When nitrogen is perceived to be a growth promoter it is usually in the form of nitrate, which is one-quarter nitrogen and three-quarters oxygen. When there is no oxygen, nitrogen does not make grass grow. Effluent becomes more effective and less smelly when it contains more oxygen. Amendments using nutrients in living form maintain the health of the soil, plants and animals. All nutrients should pass through soil biology before going to plants for optimum effectiveness.

Flowforms are commonly used in biodynamics to accentuate the effectiveness of the biodynamic preparations.

MECHANICAL & RHYTHMICAL AERATION OF EFFLUENT

Aeration can be increased further by cycling effluent through machines that increase oxygen saturation to its optimum point. One of these mechanisms is a flowform[1] that generates a rhythmical flow pattern while incorporating the oxygen. This will reduce odors, speed up decomposition, and reduce the biological oxygen demand so that the effluent can be put back on the pasture to enhance plant and soil growth. The more biology there is, the better nutrients can be absorbed and stabilized. Circulate the effluent through a flowform for about eight hours then spray it back on the pasture. This process has been seen to increase dissolved oxygen to 12 ppm. Increasing the oxygen decreases the biological oxygen demand at the point of application. I have personally observed increased growth that I would have previously thought impossible.

---

1 Flowforms are a series of concrete or plastic moulded forms that bring about a figure 8 rhythmical flow in liquid circulated through them. They were invented by John Wilkes to enliven and heal water. See *www.flowform.net*.

Biodynamic preparations being sprayed in a pasture.

A new machine has been developed by Steve Erickson on Chaos Springs Farm in New Zealand that is both a stirrer and spreader. The return flow to the tank from the pump can be changed from stirring in a clockwise direction to a counterclockwise direction to create a life-enhancing rhythm. In ten minutes of alternating directional stirring, up to 12 ppm oxygenation can be achieved. Solids like fine lime and compost are held in suspension during the stirring.

TREATING CATTLE BARNS

Biodynamic preparations are ideal for treating bedding in cattle barns and the pit underneath a herd home. The most noticeable effect of using biodynamic preparations is the reduction in smells in the barn and from the liquid manure siphoned off during the winter. When ammonia smells surround cows the availability of oxygen is diminished. The availability of fresh, well-oxygenated air is important to all animals, especially cattle. Farmers only have to look on a frosty morning when the breath is visible to see how a cow draws fresh air in from in front of her and breaths out to the sides. While grazing pasture her carbon dioxide laden breath is

This photo shows infertile pasture under a fence where no cow manure has reached.

The pasture above was sprayed with liquid manure and biodynamic preparation 500, aerated through flowforms.

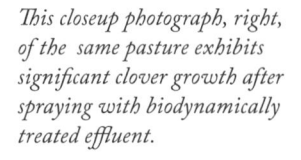

This closeup photograph, right, of the same pasture exhibits significant clover growth after spraying with biodynamically treated effluent.

breathed out into the sward, making it available to the plants to take in. Care should be taken when livestock are in confined spaces that smells from effluent do not compromise the availability of fresh air. In European cattle stalls it has been noted that the application of the biodynamic preparations to the bedding makes a significant difference to the freshness of the air. When one can smell ammonia, nitrogen is being wasted.

HIGH-RAINFALL AREAS

In areas of high rainfall where drainage may be insufficient to cope with applying effluent to the pasture, effluent ponds need to be of sufficient size to store effluent until weather and soil conditions permit the effluent to be absorbed by the soil without risk of run off.

Planting willows, poplars and flaxes (Phormiums) have been found helpful in absorbing and transpiring soil moisture. New Zealand farmers are increasingly finding that these plants serve not only to take up soil moisture but also as shelter fodder and medicine.[2] Poplars and willows grow quickly in wet areas, establish extensive root systems, and remove large quantities of water, thus drying the soil. A quick-drying soil will allow more pasture to grow and be grazed throughout the year. A mature weeping willow may transpire up to 6,600 gallons (25,000 liters) per day. Conversely, that amount of water in an arid area might well be valuable as condensate in the coolest part of the morning, as well as providing food in the form of tree leaves.

When aerated, activated effluent is spread evenly over a farm, leaching of any element is minimized while the net profit is maximized. The more widely the improved effluent is distributed on the farm, the less fertilizer is needed — to the point that the farm becomes largely self-sufficient. The less water-soluble fertilizer is applied, the better animal health becomes. With the application of these measures it is possible for a farmer to harvest all the nitrogen fertilizer needed from the air. The soil grows deeper, develops a better crumb structure, and is able to absorb more moisture and for a longer time.

---

2 From the research report, "Growing Poplar and Willow Trees on Farms," compiled and prepared by the National Poplar and Willow Users Group at *www.fao.org/forestry/21644-03ae5c141473930a1cf4b566f59b3255f.pdf*

14

It Is Being Done

SUCCESSFUL BIOLOGICAL & BIODYNAMIC GROWING
WITH HIGH YIELDS AND PROFIT

THERE are now many farmers using biological and organic systems to produce high-quality food from profitable farms. These farmers have persevered to develop systems that suit the particular soil and environmental characteristics of their farms and their own circumstances. Here are some of them.

Gavin Fisher

Gavin Fisher and his family run a small farm near Mount Te Aroha in New Zealand. Gavin describes the farm as a certified organic, solar powered, electro-magnetic energy driven, biological agricultural farming system where the ecologies and the processes of those ecologies are farmed. Gavin describes himself as a production ecologist. He has so reduced his costs through farming this way that the farm is very profitable. This type of farming system isn't reliant on organic premiums, just life forms, but Gavin is happy to take the premiums while they are offered.

The Fishers' farm has many trees, shrubs and flaxes that serve to increase the diversity of fodder as well as provide shelter from all aspects of weather extremes and enable the animals to self-medicate. It has been noted that the soil biological life changes in the pasture nearby. In the air the insect and bird life also changes. Birds eat insects and grubs making manure that is different from that of the farmed animals. Right from the beginning Gavin kept a comprehensive herb garden from which remedies could be made if needed. Asked recently about his farm veterinary expenses, he said that the biggest expense that past spring was to take a knife and cut some flax so he could treat a pock mark on a cow's teat with some of the jelly.

Early in the organic conversion stage Gavin had worm farms which were set up in bins in a manner where the leachate liquid and the vermicast solids where collected and used on the farm as part of the fertility program. The effluent from the barn is also utilized as part of the fertility program. It is often said that to be a farmer you must have something to complain about, the only complaint Gavin has is that if he leaves any fencing tools lying around the farm by mistake they get lost a lot easier these days because of the active biology and the worm castings that are getting deposited and cover up the tools. This type of farming system with all the interaction from the biological diversity is building a lot of topsoil. This must surely be one of the most carbon-positive farms in the country! Just think what a bonanza it would be if all farms were managed like this one and how much carbon tax we would collect.

Jenny & Ray Ridings

Jenny and Ray Ridings have a farm that is on reclaimed marsh, so is mainly on clay-peat soil. When I first saw it while collecting soil samples the low, flat, boggy land had turned to "concrete" in the summer. It was very short of many elements especially lime. Over the years the missing elements have been supplied with effluent and compost from the winter stand-off pad, an outdoor piped, covered pad for the cattle to lie on in winter. Now, 12 years since converting it to an organic system, the black topsoil is more than twice as deep and the clay is fracturing and breaking up well below the surface. It was once a challenge to get a willow cutting to grow and now most types of trees grow well.

Recently, following a late drought, the Ridings' farm was bare at the beginning of winter. After applying the biodynamic preparations in homeopathic form the cows were able to comfortably remain on a paddock for three days instead of two. They were less hungry and therefore trampled less grass and compacted less soil and therefore the grass was able to re-grow significantly faster. By the time they calved in the spring there was sufficient grass for them to produce very well.

At an early stage of their conversion to organic, dirty cow tails were an issue at milking time — as they are on most dairy farms. It is not

A healthy, contented herd is easy to recognize when present, as seen on Ray & Jenny Ridings' farm. When the energy balance and flow are right, better nutrition is achieved.

pleasant being hit in the face by a cow's tail holding a pound of hard lumpy manure (as well perhaps as the most recent application). In one enlightened moment Jenny said, "Do you know I think we are approaching this issue from the wrong end! Rather than trimming their tails we should be changing their diet!" This observation led to many changes on the farm over the years.

One of the trials and tribulations Jenny and Ray faced was being told that the farm needed lime, and lots of it. They now know that no element is an island to itself and that the application of one element affects all the others. With lots of patience, though, they were successful, as it took some years to bring the other elements back into balance with the added lime.

Steve & Jenny Eriksen

Steve and Jenny Eriksen have successfully used biodynamic practices to manage weeds, improve fertility, and grow very healthy young dairy cattle on their small hill farm near Waihi, New Zealand. When I first visited their farm it turned yellow in the summer with gorse and ragwort (*Jacobaea vulgaris*) flowers, as did the little farm I had near Otorohanga in 1971. A decade later such flowers are few and far between. On this farm teas are made from biodynamic compost, ragwort and gorse plants and are applied several times a year. Year after year the pasture and animal condition improved and the weeds became fewer and fewer. All through this time Steve, who is very handy in the workshop, was thinking out better and better designs for machines to brew and spread liquid fertilizers. The most recent is a machine that will stir and spread at the same time. The stirring oxygenates the brew very well so that the organisms have enough oxygen to breed and grow well. The stirring and oxygenation continues on the journey to the paddock and while the spray is being applied. This machine can also be used for a number of other tasks around the farm like water trough cleaning and fluid transport.

Yvonne & James Killaea

On another farm, owned by Yvonne and James Killaea, this machine is used to mix and spread effluent from the cowshed. To the effluent are added a little of a proprietary homeopathic biodynamic preparations product, compost and fine lime. These are given a good stir to incorporate them all together and then applied to the pasture at about 107 gallons per acre (1,000 litres per hectare). Their grass grows as well as on the best of the nearby farms that apply nitrogenous fertilizer. The added bonus is that this soil is also growing in depth and crumb structure and with plenty of worm casting on the surface. The cost is so little that I consider the use of this machine is like having a license to print money! The largest part of the fertilizer is what most people consider a waste that must be disposed of and James and Yvonne are transforming it into a very valuable fertilizer at a very low cost.

James and Yvonne Killalea became convinced that biodynamics could help them improve productivity and they have made the effort to learn about it and apply the principles very successfully to their farm near Huntly, New Zealand. Many dairy farmers think it is too difficult to introduce a regime of spraying biodynamic preparations because there is a timing clash between the ideal time for spraying and miking the cows, but James and Yvonne have found a way. They apply a preparation combination spray quarterly, and a preparation 501-based spray any time there is a need. Preparation 501 has been found to be very effective if cows start getting bloat unexpectedly.

On a recent field day on their farm, during a wet part of the winter, we noted that treated pastures were dryer and busy with casting worms. The pasture had been sprayed with a homeopathic spray based on biodynamic preparations that is designed to enhance photosynthesis. The cows in a hilly paddock came over to see us, put on a dance for us, and then came up for a scratch. They were very well fed and due to calve in a few weeks. When we left they stood back from the gate making no suggestion that they might like to leave as well. Most cows at that time of year are very cold and hungry and always on the look-out for more to eat. It was a pleasure to see such happy, healthy cows. During the season they have rewarded James and Yvonne well with very good production. The grass has grown so well that they have also been able to make at least two seasons worth of hay and silage. I consider it wise to have extra stored fodder so when a dry season comes along there is still plenty of fodder to eat.

Joel Salatin

Polyface Farm in Virginia is a modern example of what farms used to be like in Europe over a hundred years ago. In a number of ways it is a model of what a biodynamic farm should be — a diamond of many facets. The farm has a personality and is the identity of the Salatin family. On it there is a broad range of animals supporting each other. This enables an income and the variety of enterprises keep an extended family profitably busy, each with an area of responsibility, while all are cooperating as a single enterprise. There is pasture, gardens and forest giving a good balance of plant types and environment for both domestic and wild animals and other wildlife. The woodlands provide fuel for cooking and heating as well as buildings to shelter people, animals and equipment. In its diversity it is a contained whole, a balanced individuality.

It was a pleasure to have Joel Salatin visit New Zealand sowing the seeds of a great way of farming into the minds and hearts of a number

Animal diversity is evident at the Salatins' Polyface Farm. Cattle and chickens graze the same pastures in rotation.

of New Zealand farmers. I hope many of the seeds germinate and are nurtured to become mighty forest giants in the future.

Imagine the diversity and richness of farms if all farmers followed the lead these farmers have set and develop their own farm biological potentials.

15

How Biodynamics & Mineral Balancing Could Transform Farming and the Food Supply in the Future

Through balancing soil minerals, applying biodynamic preparations, and activating soil biology we now have the means to produce high-quality food. With more buyers seeking high-quality, nutritious farm products the market opportunities are present. My vision is to see biodynamics become a mainstream practice on farms, and understood by the person in the street as a logical, common-sense system, flexible enough to meet all farming needs. Then most people would have the opportunity to eat good, nutritious food. That was Rudolf Steiner's aim when he agreed to give the series of lectures to farmers which we now call the *Agriculture Course.*

Humans and animals are best suited to taking minerals from the plant world. Plants take their minerals from the soil biology that dissolves the minerals from the rock particles in the soil. The correct place to apply our mineral dietary supplements is to the soil as ground rock, not in salt form. Plant nutrients should be made available via the organisms in the soil rather than being dependent upon water solubility as has been popular for our fertilizer practices for the last hundred years or so. When we depend on water solubility we focus on one or two elements that can at times become excessively available, causing deficiencies in others, which in turn leads to deficiency diseases in plants and animals. When we work with biology, plants are able to access a much greater range of nutrients over a much greater time frame. With water solubility you change the baby with the bathwater. We need to be able to keep the baby (our soil nutrients) through many changes of water. This will greatly assist us to achieve much cleaner water run-offs from our properties.

When minerals are well balanced in the soil a suitable environment is formed for the soil biology. Soil biology also need plant and animal manure residues as part of their food supply plus enough moisture and air in the soil to survive. Adding mineral salts so that plants can take them up in the soil water has led to a degradation of quality in food plants. I grew up with the idea that adding any mineral salts was to be avoided, but found that biodynamics on mineral-deficient soils did not give good results either. I have found that adding minerals according to the teaching of Dr. William Albrecht is needed before biodynamics can have its full effect. He taught that the right relationship is vital and that the ratios need to be adjusted according to the crops one wishes to grow.

It is important that we grow food that is fit for human beings, rather than grow food that is a magnet for insects and pathogens.

Regular observation of your soil, pasture and animal conditions enables you to be proactive and correct imbalances before they lead to pest and disease problems. Through the wise use of mineral balancing and the biodynamic preparations the optimal levels and diversity of sugars, oils, proteins and vitamins can be achieved. These are important elements for the sound nutrition of animals and humans. Optimum nutrition can be achieved at every level from mineral to biology to plant to animal and finally to human. In such a system disease pathogens, parasites, pest insects and many animals that may be termed pests do not find the niche they require to pose difficulties to the farmer or grower. High-quality crops and a minimal stress environment keep animals and humans healthy at low cost.

So many farmers have been put off of organic farming by the fear that they will not be able to control weeds and pests. But when we respect those pests and weeds as indicators of what is wrong rather than as enemies we can then change the conditions so that they are no longer a problem.

Using mineral balancing and biodynamics requires thinking for yourself and developing your farm as a unique system suited to your particular conditions. When a farm has been managed well in a biodynamic system for some years it develops its own unique character or "individuality" which is appropriate for the particular climate, soil and other features of that farm. In a farm individuality, all the bodies that make up a whole being should be in balance with each other and each body should be in balance within itself to make up a healthy, happy environment that is prosperous in all senses of the word. You can use the biodynamic preparations like "organs" to achieve this.

In the *Agricultural Course* lectures, Dr. Rudolf Steiner emphasized the effects of silica, oxygen, carbon, clay and calcium, which are the main elements that make up our natural world. Most other elements farmers work with are needed in the merest trace while carbon, silica, clay and calcium are needed in gross amounts. Biodynamics helps us to manage and activate those elements. The biodynamic preparations play an important part in enhancing soil biological activity and support activity of elements like calcium, potassium, sulfur, silica, hydrogen and phosphorus.

We need much more of a focus on oxygenating the soil and our fertilizers and ensuring that there is sufficient calcium, which is stabilized in the soil if we also add carbon. Once we have this sound foundation we can use the biodynamic quartz preparation to assist plants to take in more light and thus convert sugars and nitrates to high-quality proteins and oils.

Getting your farm activated and properly balanced is more of a challenge on the many large, single-enterprise New World farms that exist on soils with low basic fertility. But it can be done, as shown by several enterprising farmers. Diversity can be provided by planting trees, including herbs and several grass varieties in pasture, and keeping additional animal types such as poultry and free-range pigs. Where the logistics of stirring and spreading biodynamic preparations are too difficult, homeopathic sprays made from biodynamic preparations and radionics can be used instead.

Each of the biodynamic preparations brings a particular energy, all of which are needed for a well-balanced dynamic farm. Introducing the energies of the biodynamic compost preparations can be done in various ways, through large-scale composting, liquid manures or cow-manure heaps. To be effective, it is important to construct heaps that conserve, rather than dissipate energy. The compost preparations and mechanical introduction of oxygen and rhythm can turn what is otherwise wasted or leached, such as dairy effluent, into valuable fertilizer.

I see a major switch emerging as more farmers see the futility of being a "more-on" farmer and realize that they can activate entire armies of workers in their soils, the various soil organisms that make up the soil food web. Through energizing plants using the biodynamic preparations, the light energy that continually rains onto the Earth can be activated and cycled through plants to feed these armies. It is quite possible and cost effective.

Mineral balancing and biodynamics provide the tools to enable farmers wishing to farm in a more sustainable way to do so successfully and profitably. We can feed the world this way! We can produce food that feeds the soul, not just the stomach, food that helps people to think clearly, stay healthy and keep smiling.

Resources

Acres U.S.A.
P.O. Box 301209, Austin, Texas 78703-0021
PHONE: 512-892-4400
FAX: 512-892-4448
EMAIL: info@acresusa.com
WEBSITE: www.acresusa.com

Bio-Dynamic Agricultural Association of Australia
c/o Post Office, Powelltown, Victoria 3797 Australia
PHONE: 61-03-5966-7333
FAX: 61-03-5966-7433
WEBSITE: www.demeter.org.au

Biodynamic Farming & Gardening Association
P.O. Box 944, East Troy, Wisconsin 53120-0944
PHONE: 262-649-9212
FAX: 262-649-9213
EMAIL: info@biodynamics.com
WEBSITE: www.biodynamics.com

Biodynamic Farming & Gardening Association in Australia
P.O. Box 54, Bellingen, New South Wales 2454 Australia
PHONE: 02-6655-0566
FAX: 02-6655-0565
EMAIL: bdoffice@biodynamics.net.au
WEBSITE: www.biodynamics.net.au

Bio Dynamic Farming & Gardening Association in New Zealand
P.O. Box 39045, Wellington, New Zealand
PHONE: 64-4-589-5366
FAX: 64-4-589-5365
EMAIL: info@biodynamic.org.nz
WEBSITE: www.biodynamic.org.nz

Biodynamic Growing magazine
P.O. Box 5018, Cranbourne Park, Victoria 3977 Australia
EMAIL: bdgrowing@dcsi.net.au
WEBSITE: www.bdgrowing.com

Brookside Laboratories, Inc.
308 South Main St., New Knoxville, OH 45871
PHONE: 419-753-2448
FAX: 419-753-2949
WEBSITE: www.blinc.com

Demeter Association, Inc.
P.O. Box 1390, Philomath, Oregon 97370
PHONE: 541-929-7148
EMAIL: jim@demeter-usa.org
WEBSITE: www.demeter-usa.org

Demeter Biodynamic Trade Association
P.O. Box 264, Talmage, California 95481-0264
EMAIL: info@demeterbta.com
WEBSITE: www.demeterbta.com

Josephine Porter Institute for Applied Biodynamics, Inc.
P.O. Box 133, Woolwine, Virginia 24185-0133
PHONE: 276-930-2463
FAX: 276-930-2475
EMAIL: info@jpidynamics.org
WEBSITE: www.jpibiodynamics.org

Rudolf Steiner College, A Center for Biodynamic Education
9200 Fair Oaks Blvd., Fair Oaks, California 95628-6811
PHONE: 916-961-8727
FAX: 877-782-1884
EMAIL: rsc@steinercollege.edu
WEBSITE: www.steinercollege.edu

The Pfeiffer Center
260 Hungry Hollow Road, Chestnut Ridge, New York 10977-6304
PHONE: 845-352-5020
EMAIL: info@pfeiffercenter.org
WEBSITE: www.pfeiffercenter.org

Yggdrasil Land Foundation
1002A O'Reilly Ave., San Francisco, California 94129-1101
PHONE: 415-561-6162
EMAIL: info@yggdrasillandfoundation.org
WEBSITE: www.yggdrasillandfoundation.org

Index

Achillea millefolium, 30
aerobic organisms, 16
Agriculture Course, 9, 48, 57, 70, 72, 78, 88, 135, 137
Agriculture of Tomorrow, 96
Albrecht, William A., *x*, 25-26, 46, 106-107
alpaca, 120
aluminum, 91
ammonia smells, 125
ammonium, 41-42
Andersen, Arden, *x-xi*, 32
animal health, 113-121
animal peppering, 107-112
anions, 27
antioxidants, 8
astral body, 70, 104
bacteria, in soil, 15-16
barber pole worm, 117-118
barrel manure, 77, 87-88
BD 500, *x*, 50, 57, 59-66, 68, , 74, 119-121, 105-106

BD 501, 30, 57, 59-62, 64-66, 68, 75, 105-106, 119-121
BD 502, 30, 78-79, 85
BD 503, 74, 79-80, 85
BD 504, 80, 85
BD 505, 80-81, 85
BD 506, 73, 81, 85
BD 507, 82, 85
BD 508, 90, 106
BD compost starter, 53
beef animals, 20
beef, corn-fed, 2
beef, pasture-fed, 2
bicarbonate of soda, 119
biodynamic preparations, 34, 49, 59, 73, 137
biodynamic, 49, 53-57
biodynamics, 48, 50, 52-56, 69
bloat, 119
boron, 27, 33, 36
Brassicas, 31
Bray 2 phosphorus test, 66

brix, 62
Brookside Laboratories, 28, 33, 66
buttercups, 108
calcium pectate, 32
calcium process, 57-58
calcium, 8, 17, 31, 33-34, 41, 43-44, 57-58, 121
calcium, deficiency, 32
calcium, energy, 106
Callahan, Philip, 39
calving, 37
carbon cycle, 13
carbon, 14, 16, 44-45
castings, earthworm, 18-19, 20
cations, 26
cattle barns, 125
certified organic, 23
chamomile, 73, 79-80
Chaos Springs Farm, 125
chlorine, 27, 35
clay, 91
clay soils, 25
Clearwater's Organic Dairy, 2
cobalt, 27, 36, 44, 91, 118
complex sugars, 8
compost, 1, 77, 83-87
compost pile, 84
compost tea, 18, 47, 50, 94
compost turner, 86
copper sulfate, 119
copper, 36, 118

cow horns, 60
cow manure heap, 89
cow pat pit, 87-90
dairy cow, 20
dandelion, 81
diamagnetic, 31, 68
disease, 103-112
diversity, 137
dolomite, 29
drainage, 19
drench, 119
dry cows, 120-121
Earth, 71
earthworm, 32
earthworm castings, 18-19, 20
effluent, 123-127
ego, 104
Emoto, Masuru, 7
equisetum, 90
Eriksen, Steve and Jenny, 125, 131
essential amino acids, 8
essential oils, 7
etheric body, 70, 103-104
fertility balancing, 113
fertilizers, acid-based, 24
fish fertilizer, 34, 50
Fisher, Gavin, 129
flowforms, 124
full moon, 98
Fuller's rose weevil, 108
fungi, 17

Germany, 47
goats, 20
grass, bitterness, 68
grass, sweet, 68
grass species, diversity, 114-115
gypsum, 29
haylage, 119
health, animal, 113-121
herbs, 114
herbs, medicinal, 7
Hoemonchus contortus, 117-118
homeopathic preparations of BD preps, 74-75
homeopathy, 27, 72
horn clay, 90-91
horn manure preparation, *x*, 50, 57, 59-66, 68, , 74, 119-121, 105-106
horn quartz preparation, 30, 57, 59-62, 64-66, 68, 75, 105-106, 119-121
horn silica preparation, *see horn quartz*
horses, 20
humic acid, 44
humus, 18, 40, 44, 84, 91
hydrogen, 14, 16
hypocalcemia, 121
Ingham, Elaine, 14-15
insect peppering, 111-112
iodine, 27, 33, 37
iron, 35, 91

Jacobaea vulgaris, 97-102
Jupiter, 58, 71
Killaea, Yvonne and James, 132
Kolisko, Lily and Eugen, 72, 96
leaching, 39
leaky gut syndrome, 6
Liebig, Justus von, 23-24, 42
lime, 25, 29, 33, 84
liquid manures, 90
livestock health, 23
Loch Arthur Community, 2
Lovel, Hugh, 69
magnesium, 8, 29, 34, 41, 44
magnesium, deficiency, 120
manganese, 35
manure, liquid, 34
Marama Organic Farm, 2
Mars, 58, 71
Mehlich 3 phosphorus test, 66
Mercury, 58, 71
milk fever, 121
Mills, Nick, 47
Millton, James and Annie, 2
minerals, in fruits and vegetables, 8
molybdenum, 27, 33, 36
molybdenum, excess, 119
moon planting calendar, 72
moon, 58, 71
moon, full, 98
muriate of potash, 24
mycorrhyzal fungi, 17

nitrate, 8, 16, 27, 33, 39, 43, 123
nitrifying bacteria, 45
nitrites, 16
nitrogen leaching, 43
nitrogen, 16, 24, 39-40, 42, 45, 115
NPK, 8, 24
nutrients, water-soluble, 24
oak bark, 80-81
omega-3 fatty acids, 7, 9
omega-6 fatty acids, 9
organic, certified, 23
organic matter, 14
organs, 69
oxygen, 14, 16, 39
paramagnetic, 31, 68
Paramagnetism, 39
passion vine hopper, 108
pasture pulling, 30
pepper, ragwort, 97-102
peppering, animal, 107-112
peppering, insects, 111-112
peppering, plant, 96-102
pest management, 106-112
pests, 103-112
Pfeiffer, Ehrenfried E., 9, 52-56
pH, 26, 30, 42-43
phosphorus, x, 8, 17, 27-28, 32, 36, 68, 118
photosynthesis, 13-14, 66
physical body, 70
plant light processes, 67

plant peppering, 96-102
Polyface Farm, 133
pore spaces, in soil, 16
possum skin ash, 108-111
potash, 25
potassium, 8, 25-26, 29-30, 35, 41, 44, 91
potentizing, 89-99
Pottenger, Francis M., 3
protein, 16
quartz crystals, 30, 60
rabbits, 108
radionics, 74-75
ragwort, 97-102, 108
ragwort pepper, 97-102
rainfall, high, 127
Ridings, Jenny and Ray, 130
Rippon Vineyard and Winery, 48
rock powder, 21, 84
rumen fermentation, 29
Salatin, Joel, 2, 133
sandy soil, 29
Saturn, 58, 71
scale and leaf roller, 108
Schwartz, Max Karl (M.K.), 90-91
seaweed, 34, 50, 84, 94
selenium, 27, 33, 37
sheep, 20
silica process, 58
silica, 8, 91

sodium, 26, 30, 35, 44
soft feet, 121
soil, sandy, 29
soil acidity, 25
soil amendments, 23
Soil Biology Primer, 14-15
soil biology, 13, 25, 34
soil food web, 14-15
soil organisms, 18
soil silica, 67
soil tests, 24
Stegemann, Ernst, 91
Steiner, Rudolf, *ix*, 9-10, 46-49, 55, 57, 70, 72, 91, 137
stinging nettle, 80
stress, livestock, 116
sugars, 14, 34
sulfate, 29
sulfur, 16, 27, 31, 36
sunlight, 16
superphosphate, 28-29
thatch, 19
Thun, Maria, 88, 112
trace elements, 27, 45
trees, in pastures, 114
urea, 41
valerian, 82
Venus, 58, 71, 109-110
vineyard, biodynamic, 47
vitamin D, 68, 121
vitamin E, 37
vitamins, 8

weed management, 93-102
weed tea, 95
weeds, 21, 93-102
Wheeler, Phil, *x*, 32
whitefly, 108
windrow, 85-87
worm farms, 77, 82
xylem cells, 67
yarrow, 30, 78-79
zinc, 27, 36, 44, 121

Acres U.S.A. — books are just the beginning!

Farmers and gardeners around the world are learning to grow bountiful crops profitably — without risking their own health and destroying the fertility of the soil. *Acres U.S.A.* can show you how. If you want to be on the cutting edge of organic and sustainable growing technologies, techniques, markets, news, analysis and trends, look to *Acres U.S.A.* For over 40 years, we've been the independent voice for eco-agriculture. Each monthly issue is packed with practical, hands-on information you can put to work on your farm, bringing solutions to your most pressing problems. Get the advice consultants charge thousands for . . .

- Fertility management
- Non-chemical weed & insect control
- Specialty crops & marketing
- Grazing, composting & natural veterinary care
- Soil's link to human & animal health

For a free sample copy or to subscribe, visit us online at
www.acresusa.com
or call toll-free in the U.S. and Canada
1-800-355-5313

Outside U.S. & Canada call 512-892-4400
fax 512-892-4448 • info@acresusa.com